Love and Objectivity in Virtue Ethics:
Aristotle, Lonergan, and Nussbaum on Emotions and Moral Insight

Since the Enlightenment, a great deal of ethical philosophy has presumed that rational human beings must set aside their emotions when seeking to make objective and sound moral decisions. *Love and Objectivity in Virtue Ethics* challenges this presumption, arguing that emotions such as compassion and love are powerful aids in the complex process of attaining objective moral truths.

Drawing on Aristotle's *Nicomachean Ethics* and the work of Bernard Lonergan and Martha Nussbaum, Robert J. Fitterer tests the assumption that the inclusion of the emotions leads to bias, thereby making it impossible to reach objective judgments or to determine moral truths. Fitterer first demonstrates how certain cognitive operations set out in Aristotelian virtue ethics can indeed arrive at objective moral truth precisely through the contribution emotions make to moral discernment. Second, drawing on Lonergan's notion of inductive insight, he argues that objectivity is the result of the properly functioning subjectivity of a moral agent. Finally, building on Nussbaum's ethical writings, Fitterer concludes that compassionate love is an attitude that actually fosters the likelihood of discerning and choosing the genuine good and encourages objectivity in moral decision-making.

Richly detailed and carefully argued, *Love and Objectivity in Virtue Ethics* is a convincing study that brings together the work of three important writers on ethics, and a passionate appeal to re-examine the process by which humans genuinely make vitally important decisions.

(Lonergan Studies)

ROBERT J. FITTERER is the senior pastor at Emmanuel Baptist Church, Victoria, and teaches philosophy at the William Carey Institute.

ROBERT J. FITTERER

Love and Objectivity in Virtue Ethics

Aristotle, Lonergan, and Nussbaum on Emotions and Moral Insight

UNIVERSITY OF TORONTO PRESS
Toronto Buffalo London

Toronto Buffalo London
www.utppublishing.com
Printed in the U.S.A.

Reprinted in paperback 2015

ISBN 978-0-8020-9788-0 (cloth)
ISBN 978-1-4875-2005-2 (paper)

Printed on acid-free paper

Lonergan Studies

Library and Archives Canada Cataloguing in Publication

Fitterer, Robert J. (Robert John), 1959–
Love and objectivity in virtue ethics : Aristotle, Lonergan, and Nussbaum on emotions and moral insight / Robert J. Fitterer.

(Lonergan studies)
Includes bibliographical references and index.
ISBN 978-0-8020-9788-0 (bound). – ISBN 978-1-4875-2005-2 (paperback)

1. Aristotle. 2. Lonergan, Bernard J.F. (Bernard Joseph Francis), 1904–1984. 3. Nussbaum, Martha Craven, 1947–. 4. Virtue. 5. Objectivity. 6. Love – Philosophy. 7. Emotions. I. Title. II. Series: Fitterer, Robert J. (Robert John), 1959– Lonergan Studies.

BJ1012.F548 2008 179'9 C2008-900505-8

This book has been published with the help of a grant from the Canadian Federation for the Humanities and Social Sciences, through the Aid to Scholarly Publications Programme, using funds provided by the Social Sciences and Humanities Research Council of Canada.

University of Toronto Press acknowledges the financial support for its publishing activities of the Government of Canada through the Canada Book Fund.

Canada Council for the Arts Conseil des Arts du Canada

ONTARIO ARTS COUNCIL
CONSEIL DES ARTS DE L'ONTARIO
an Ontario government agency
un organisme du gouvernement de l'Ontario

University of Toronto Press acknowledges the financial assistance to its publishing program of the Canada Council for the Arts and the Ontario Arts Council, an agency of the Government of Ontario.

Contents

Acknowledgments

This book would not have been possible without the guidance of wise and caring people who played key roles in my academic journey. I wish, therefore, to thank David Widdicombe for encouraging me to do theological study; Stan Grenz for urging me on to doctoral work; Ivan Gaetz for introducing me to Lonergan's thought; Eike-Henner Kluge for introducing me to Aristotle and Aquinas; and finally Mortimer Adler, who personally gave me a last homework assignment before he retired, a study in semiotics and the philosophy of language.

I also wish to thank mentors at the University of British Columbia Department of Philosophy for their guidance as I developed the ideas in this book, especially Jim Dybikowski, Paul Bartha, and Andrew Irvine. It was an honour, as well, to have Kenneth Melchin of Saint Paul University, Ottawa, as a most enthusiastic supporter of this project.

My wife, Casey, and my children, Sarah, Adam, and Jenny, deserve infinite gratitude for putting up with those many times when I had to be away studying and writing. Through their faith, hope, and love they have made this work possible.

Love and Objectivity in Virtue Ethics

Introduction

This book is an inquiry into the kind of objectivity proper to Aristotelian virtue ethics. In such an ethics, the grasp of what is good or right in a given scenario is said to be attainable through some kind of moral sensitivity that operates, at least in part, directly from an agent's feelings, life experience, and empathic sensitivity to concrete situations. The virtuous person has acquired skill in spotting ethical salience in particular cases. But it is here, seemingly, that the influence of bias, special interest, and poor cognition may interfere. For how reliable can an ethics be that is grounded in the idiosyncrasies of human subjectivity? In what follows, I hope to give a convincing description of a functional dynamic in our ethical living that may rightly be called 'being objective.' I seek to show that the objectivity appropriate for a virtue ethics is a by-product of well-functioning cognitive processes described by philosopher and theologian Bernard Lonergan. Furthermore, I hope to demonstrate, in the light of philosopher and classicist Martha Nussbaum's recent work, how emotions and desires play an indispensable part in fostering this objectivity-promoting process. To put it in Aristotelian terms, I seek to show that living well requires loving aright.

Since Aristotle offers the classic exemplar of virtue ethics, I will interact with his thought throughout this project. In his *Nicomachean Ethics,* Aristotle argues that it is the 'person of practical wisdom' – the *phronimos*[1] – who has become an expert at sound ethical deliberation and action. This person is described as someone who, while knowing, say, that courage and generosity are virtues, is still only able to determine which of these might be the overriding moral concern by attending to the particular case, and by considering his or her own connection to that case. Moreover, the ethical salience detectable in any given case is properly grasped only when the practically wise person's cognitive capacities have not been distorted by untrained emotion or a love of base things. The development of such practical intelligence (*phronesis*) and moral virtue (*aretê ethike*) comes about through a continuing interaction with actual life situations and the shape of our emotive and intellectual responses to them.

Right here we sense a difficulty, one that arises, it seems, because modern Western culture is beholden to a notion of objectivity ascribed to the empirical and theoretical sciences – bracketed emotions, identically trained colleagues, accurate and widely accepted standards of measurement, theoretical laws, absolute constants, mathematical degrees of certainty, and so forth. These are popular images of applied scientific method. But no end of difficulty has resulted from seeking to apply to ethics the objectivity proper to the hard sciences. Ethically charged decisions, such as which books I should permit my young children to read, do not obviously call for such criteria as absolute precision, consensus among all parents, or inference from theoretical descriptions of the good or the right. What is needed here is a distinction between the kind of objectivity proper to the hard sciences and that proper to ethics.

In a virtue ethics, it is a unique mode of intelligence, working within a kind of experience-based moral perception, that would determine a right choice (*phronesis*), and it is hard to see why this method should have to answer to scientific criteria. But how would we justify the conclusions and choices of a perception-based mode of gaining particularist moral insights? If ethics were simply a matter of logical deductions, objectivity would be grounded in the self-evidence of moral first principles and the reliability of the rules of inference. But perceptions are notoriously fallible things, especially if we expect them to be affected by emotions, disposition, and habits.

All these concerns indicate that at least two questions regarding the cognitive side of an Aristotelian ethics have not been finally settled and, with the renewed interest in virtue ethics, are still worth pursuing. First, viewed from the inside, from the perspective of the subject, what is the nature of the cognitive activity going on within the *phronimos* – the practically wise person – when he is 'getting it right' in moral discernment and deliberation? Second, since, according to Aristotle, practical wisdom requires some reliance upon criteria that may be interpreted as subjective, such as the agent's situational context and emotive interaction, what do we mean when we say that a given agent is 'being objective' in this process?

In treating the second of these questions, my project here is not to develop a full-blown theory of ethical objectivity, one that will compete with other such theories and yet be distinct from scientific objectivity. Rather, I am going to focus upon a specific weakness of virtue theories like Aristotle's; namely, the dangers of personal bias. These dangers can be addressed,

I think, not by eliminating subjective factors but by properly understanding them and harnessing them. Part of the answer is intended to show that emotion can be a corrective to bias rather than merely one of its causes.

In treating the first question, I head in a direction set by some recent studies in cognitive psychology, a direction that promises to be useful for understanding the inner processes of moral decision making. These processes include an acquired deliberative expertise that gains *Gestalt*-like insight directly from situational appearances.[2] Such a decision-making skill does not entirely eliminate the role of calculation, deduction, and application of rules and procedures, but banks on a qualitative change that occurs when novices become experts at problem solving. This change is an ability to 'act without thinking' or to just 'see what needs doing' in a way analogous to how a chess master 'sees' the right move without having mentally to exhaust the set of all possible moves.[3]

Much excellent work has already been done in regard to the processes of particularist discernment and practical insight induction.[4] A relatively unknown scholar, however, and one whose work is a good entry point for a more scientifically informed moral psychology is the late Canadian Jesuit philosopher Bernard Lonergan (1904–84).[5] Among his many works are two seminal ones, *Insight: A Study of Human Understanding* (1957) and *Method in Theology* (1971). In the former, the Aristotelian-Thomist tradition of Catholic thought is modified and brought into serious encounter with empirical scientific method and the statistical method of the soft sciences and genetics. Lonergan puts the venerable tradition on a somewhat neo-Kantian footing that relies on the foundation of certain prior mental operations that make knowledge possible in the first place, and that are the only recourse for justifying our beliefs and decisions. In his later *Method in Theology* he asserts, among other things, a cognitive role for the emotions and their inseparability from responsible action and rational thinking. For Lonergan, knowledge is an ongoing developmental structure, involving the whole person and including the intersubjective and collaborative social world. The inception and development of knowledge moves through a dialectical interaction of the agent with the phenomenal world. The world does not simply impress itself upon us; neither do we project or construct the world. Rather, the agent goes back and forth between the particular data of presentation, insight, and judgment and returns again to presentation, spiralling upward in a self-correcting process of learning. This dialectic is captured in Lonergan's claim that 'genuine objectivity is the achievement of authentic subjectivity.'[6]

For both Lonergan and Aristotle, determining an ethical truth will require a turning to concrete presentations and the inspection of real contexts and situations. Clearly, such inspection will engage our emotions, past experiences, hunches, memories, sudden insights, symbols, imaginary cases, and acquired rules of thumb. But these factors must be *deliberately* and *intelligently* engaged, not arbitrarily, accidentally, or nonchalantly. For we intuit this much at least: that it is not morally praiseworthy to copy our peers thoughtlessly or to let indifference characterize our choices and actions, for deliberation and choice entangle us in real responsibility.

Aristotle seems to be pointing at this requirement when he claims that a morally praiseworthy act must be done in full awareness of *what* we are doing and *why* we do it. It must be an act freely chosen and not done from coercion. To think and deliberate well is something we can choose to do, or at least desire to do, and hence sound cognitive functioning, insofar as we can self-consciously take hold of it, becomes an ethically charged concern. We are morally obliged not only to *act* well but to *think* well, too.

There is, then, a kind of sober self-appropriation wherein the subject, aware of the fact that she is in a deliberative process, takes hold to some degree of the stages of that process precisely to promote a sound and responsible outcome. This is the subject operating well as a *self-conscious* subject to overcome limitation and head towards objectivity and moral truth. At least one of the most vital stages of such a self-appropriation is awareness of and compensation for personal bias, the prejudices that would deceive the very discernment she is trying to bring to excellent development.

In this book, I argue that Lonergan's general theory of sound cognition and his analysis of its breakdown in bias can contribute to the alternative type of objectivity called for above. I show that Lonergan's mode of particularist intelligence, called 'common sense insight,' is the mode of insight deployed by Aristotle's person of practical wisdom. Thus, if *phronesis* is a species of common sense insight, I can deploy certain aspects of Lonergan's notions of objectivity and particularist insight to bolster the weaknesses of Aristotelian virtue ethics; namely, the danger of bias.

Even so, however useful Lonergan may be in the phenomenology of insight, he is in need of considerable enrichment when it comes to emotional cognition. I think Martha Nussbaum's recent work can provide this. Lonergan claims that part of what happens through our emotions is the discernment of values, and furthermore, that it is love that somehow acts as an architectonic emotion that may provide an overall viewpoint or commitment that actually promotes objective value discernment. But Lonergan did not satisfactorily flesh this out. Thus, I turn to Nussbaum, who unpacks in far greater detail the ways in which emotional intelligence operates as a mode of perception and of judgment. She too calls for some kind of love to play an indispensable role in moral insight induction. After critically adjusting some of her claims, I merge them with Lonergan's ideas in order to arrive at a practical notion of 'being objective' that addresses the bias concerns that may attend virtue ethics.

My thesis in this book, then, is that a modified account of Nussbaum's insights on love's discernment can satisfactorily fill out gaps in Lonergan's general theory of cognition and value apprehension. In turn, Lonergan's general theory and his common sense insight go a long way towards answering the two questions that guide this inquiry: just what are we doing when we gain concrete moral insight; and why should doing that be considered objective?

In the process of working this out, I will be moving beyond strict Aristotelian ethics and will present ideas applicable to a more broadly construed virtue ethics. While many notions herein discussed, such as emotional discernment or the relation between bias/preference and the phenomenal aspect of the world, are compatible extensions of Aristotle's theory, others, such as love as a controlling background emotion or healthy subjectivity as a correlative to genuine objectivity, are notions clearly outside the Aristotelian framework. Still, they represent concerns that are relevant to any modern presentation of virtue ethics, because they build into the foundational concept of human nature the legitimate contemporary concerns for evolutionary process (both social and biological), cultural and historical development, and the importance of freedom and choice in the making of one's own character.

Chapter 1 presents a short exposition of Aristotle's *Nicomachean Ethics*. That work establishes the basic elements and relations of an ethics grounded in the flourishing of human nature. It introduces such issues as the unique function of humankind, the ultimate goal of all human action, and the means necessary for attaining the good proper to human function and ends. It also introduces the elements of a practical wisdom and of an acquired state of 'right desire' (*orthos orexis*) that orients us towards the genuine good. After this exposition I take a closer look at four key themes that arise from Aristotle's treatment and to which I return throughout the project: first, the intelligent and discerning nature of our emotions and desires; second, the dialectical relationship between our desires and the way the world appears to us; third, the non-inferential mode of thinking that is at work in ethical insight; and fourth, the practical particularism that inevitably seems to result for an ethics relying upon direct insight into concrete states of affairs.

In chapter 2, I present in condensed form aspects of Bernard Lonergan's theory of the cognitive operations that we spontaneously perform in learning and knowing. I uncover the several interdependent yet distinct types of cognitive action that must be performed methodically if we are to learn and know anything at all. Beneath these acts is revealed the actor, the subject confronting the phenomenal world with desire, emotions, and the need to make decisions. Lonergan asserts a twofold role for emotions in the cognitive process: they are vital components of how we apprehend value and they inform the process of judging value. My purpose here is to set up a theoretical backdrop for a comparison of Lonergan's insight with Aristotle's *phronesis.*

Chapter 3 brings this general theory down to earth, where we see it embodied in a specialization of intelligence that Lonergan called common sense insight. Common sense is the mode of intelligence that all persons and societies develop in order successfully to cope with the ad hoc contingencies of daily living. But it also includes the concerns of personal growth and intersubjective development. Common sense is shown to share many significant traits with *phronesis*: concern with mastering the concrete decisions and actions that impinge upon us; construal of the world and illumination of ethical salience that increases with experience and expertise; allowance for emotion in the apprehension of particular value; and the corresponding problem of bias in which unsound desires and emotions distort the phenomenal field. By identifying *phronesis* as a species of common sense insight, this chapter allows me to apply aspects of Lonergan's bias discussion to the context of virtue ethics. But I think his treatment of emotive cognition is inadequate to the task of ethical insight and thus is in need of deeper input.

Therefore, in chapter 4 I turn to elements of Martha Nussbaum's recent study of emotional intelligence in order to fill in lacunae in Lonergan's emotive theory. I present her theory of emotion-as-identical-to-value-judgment; I offer what I think are necessary critiques and amendments of that theory; and then I explore the ways that some mode of love can be the emotion that overcomes, to a significant degree, the problems of bias. Both the correction for bias and the illumination of ethical salience through compassion pave the way for a notion of *performative* objectivity, a notion that I think is adequate to the task of 'getting it right' in virtue ethics.

1

Aristotle's *Nicomachean Ethics*, Books I, II, III, and VI

This book pursues two general questions. First, what have I been doing right when I make a breakthrough while pondering a moral conundrum, when the 'light goes on' and I hit upon a sound moral insight? Second, why should doing that count as 'being objective' with regard to moral truth and moral perception? In seeking an answer to these questions, I am seeking to understand both the method of doing virtue ethics as well as factors that interfere with the operations of that method. Since my whole inquiry has been instigated by intriguing and difficult doctrines found in Aristotle's works, I will begin by presenting an exposition of sections of Aristotle's *Nicomachean Ethics,* as well as important passages from his *De Anima.* These writings present a theory of how we are to live out the good human life, of what counts as the end goal of living well, and what would be the suitable means of attaining that end. The end goal of human living turns out to be a carefully defined notion of happiness (*eudaimonia*), and the means of attaining it turns out to be an equally well-defined notion of moral virtue plus practical wisdom.[1]

Aristotle's *Nicomachean Ethics* is not a speculative work that attempts to penetrate the metaphysics of 'the good' as such. It is a practical book, the goal of which is to help the reader understand and perhaps become a good human being, living well his or her own life. If there were a single question guiding Aristotle's ethics, it could be the one that Julia Annas thinks drove most ethical projects of the ancient world: *How should I live my life as a whole*?[2] To that kind of question Aristotle offers some answers based largely upon a theory of the nature and function of human beings.

Anticipating objections, Aristotle reminds the reader not to expect from ethical study the kind of epistemic precision that one might expect from, say, mathematics. The nature of the subject matter determines what degree of precision is possible, and ethical deliberation is not an exact science.[3] This cannot mean ethical relativism or scepticism, because Aristotle claims to disclose objective, rational, justifiable, and motivating truths regarding the human good. Still, ethical truth differs from scientific truth and cannot be captured in abstractions such as universally applicable moral maxims.

If, then, there is ethical truth, from where does the imprecision arise? Is it that the human good itself is ambiguous? Is it our conception of that human good that is somehow imprecise? Or does it arise from the contingent particularity of each human life? Perhaps moral imprecision arises from the method by which we are to arrive at ethical truth, or worse, from perversions of that method. My goal in this chapter is to lay bare enough of the Aristotelian ethics and cognitive psychology to show that (i) the imprecision comes from the prior indeterminacy of the concrete good relative to each individual human who must discern it, combined with (ii) the probabilistic nature of human insight when deployed in concrete problem solving. This will set the stage for my later examination of Lonergan and Nussbaum on just these issues.

Against the background of my exposition of these sections of the *Nicomachean Ethics*, I will examine special components of the Aristotelian theory of moral insight; namely, reliance upon perception, emotions, and non-inferential thinking. In doing so, I will be working with readings of the text influenced by Nancy Sherman, Martha Nussbaum, and David Wiggins. These respected commentators have offered reasonable resolutions to some difficulties in Aristotle and I wish to build on their work, not retrace their steps. I will, from time to time, move beyond explicitly Aristotelian teaching, but I suggest that my interpretations are compatible extensions of Aristotle's thought and as such deserve to be considered as legitimate viewpoints of the operations of virtue-based ethics in general.

Key Sections in the *Nicomachean Ethics*

The End of Human Action: Happiness

Aristotle opens the *Nicomachean Ethics* with a study of the nature of human action.[4] Rational human action always aims at some end. The end of an action can be called the 'good' of that action. Just as there is a plurality of human actions, whether productive, performative, or intellectual, so too there is a corresponding plurality of ends, of goods worth pursuing. Thus, health is the good at which the medical arts aim; victory the good at which strategy aims; a ship the good at which shipbuilding aims.

In addition, some pursuits can be ordered to others. For example, good horseback riding can itself be pursued in order to attain the good of military combat – victory. Health is a desirable end in itself, but it is also a part of a larger good life. Human actions, therefore, can be understood as operating within a hierarchy, with some actions as subordinate means of attaining others. The question then arises: is there a *final* end at the top of this hierarchy, an end sought for its own sake *alone*, all else being desired for the sake of this one? The question can also be put non-hierarchically: considering all human actions taken together precisely as a set, is there a single end towards which the set as a whole aims? To know this would be a great influence in living our lives, for 'shall we not, then, like archers who have a mark at which to aim, be more likely to hit upon what is right?'[5] Understanding human nature and the ends of human actions seems indispensable, then, to living a humanly good life.

Aristotle's dialectical investigation shows that people generally do have a rough idea what the final good might be: it is happiness (*eudaimonia*), and they suppose that living well (*eu zên*) and doing well (*eu prattein*) are the same as happiness. But what do these terms mean when fleshed out? Some say the highest good is pleasure, wealth, health, honour, virtue, and the like. Others, namely Platonists, say that the highest good is some self-subsisting, eternal absolute that causes the goodness in all those lesser things in which it participates.[6] Pleasure could be the final end of all activity, but only for the vulgar man and for beasts. Honour, which the noble esteem, is dependent upon others for its bestowal, and consequently is too vulnerable to loss even for good men. Virtue is certainly a great good, but it is somehow felt to be incomplete, for one could have virtue and yet be asleep or in dire poverty, and surely this could not be happiness. Money is sought for what it can buy, not as an end in itself, and so cannot constitute happiness. In this way, Aristotle goes on to remove false candidates while closing in on his own conception of the right one. Unlike the partial goods or the merely apparent goods, happiness must have at least these four characteristics: first, it must be the *final* good, sought for its own sake and never for the sake of some further goal; second, it must be a complete good, self-sufficient, and leave nothing else outside itself to be desired;[7] third, happiness will involve the full and proper operation of whatever specific functions are definitive of human being; and fourth, this full and proper functioning must not be for a mere season but must characterize our lives as a whole.[8] This preliminary definition is augmented as Aristotle proceeds.

The Function of Human Beings

Aristotle turns from teleological clarifications of happiness to the study of human nature, its capacities and operations. For if human operations, properly directed and performed, are essential to experiencing the human good, then it is necessary that we understand the most characteristic functions of human beings as such. This will mean an anthropological study of the uniquely human capacities that distinguish us from other creatures.

What is the function of the whole human being as such? Nutrition, growth, and reproductive functions we share with plants and animals; perceptual awareness we share with other animals. Unique to humans, however, is the *rational* part of the soul, and thus an expressly *human* function must be some life of activity involving that rational part.[9]

Now, this essential human function, as is the case with all capacities, may be poorly or excellently operative. The proper and full functioning of a capacity is called its excellence, its virtue (*aretê*). The excellent functioning of human rational capacity would be the excellence proper to mankind. The distinctly *human* good, then, is a psychic activity in accordance with virtue, and if there is more than one virtue, in accord with the best and the most complete of them.

Aristotle goes on dialectically to deepen and clarify his account of the human good and the well-functioning activity that constitutes it – virtue. Two further opinions of what happiness must include are considered next: there must be *some* accompanying pleasure, and there must be *some* external prosperity. Regarding prosperity, he argues that we need 'enough' external goods to act as instruments, say, for enabling noble actions. Generosity, for instance, might require a certain modicum of personal wealth – what counts as the 'right amount' ought to be left indeterminate. Children and friends are also valuable goods external to us and without which we cannot function in complete happiness. But regarding pleasure he introduces a notion that will become very important when we investigate moral perception and deliberation. To the good and noble person, pleasure is not a goal in itself, but it does *accompany* noble actions that are such goals. Aristotle captures this phenomenological fact in stating that 'to each man, that which he is said to be a lover of is pleasant.'[10] Just as a horse lover finds looking at horses pleasant, so too deeds of justice are pleasant to the lover of justice, and by extension, virtuous acts in general are pleasant to the virtuous person. For certainly no one would be called just who felt repulsed inside by the thought or performance of just actions. Whatever gives someone joy and pleasure is an indicator of that person's loves and desires; this separates virtuous characters from base ones. It also separates virtuous ones from merely continent ones. The continent person does the right thing, but in a forced and joyless manner.

A somewhat more detailed definition of the human good – happiness (*eudaimonia*) – can now be given: 'The happy person is the one who expresses complete virtue in his activities, with an adequate supply of external goods, not just for a time but for a complete life.'[11] This condition is a stable disposition not easily altered and never completely lost.[12]

Human Virtue

Since *eudaimonia* is an activity expressing complete virtue, we must examine the various excellences that the human soul can manifest. The part of the soul that seems rationally improvable towards functional excellence is the desiring and emotive (orectic) part.[13] For not all desires respond to training or to belief: appetites of the body, such as hunger, are not tameable in this way. But intentional desires and responsive emotions – preferences, fears, delights, and all those drives that bid us to pursue or flee some object or goal – while springing initially from a pre-critical state of our development, do respond to beliefs and can be influenced until they are predisposed to pursue proper objects in the proper way. The person whose appetites and desires are so tempered is the one we praise for having good character.[14]

The orectic part of the soul has the capacity to be habituated, through pedagogy and practice, until it desires spontaneously the things that it ought.[15] Consciously or not, we build habits of preference and action by choosing and implementing activities of a certain kind; we grow through developmental stages in which some tendencies of choice and some preferences are acquired and strengthened, others discouraged or eliminated. The result is a developed set of tendencies that we call either virtue or vice, depending upon whether these tendencies become constitutive of or repugnant to *eudaimonia*. Aristotle says, therefore, that we are not born virtuous, but by learning to *do* acts of justice we will *become* just, and by learning to *feel* fear or confidence in the right circumstances we will *become* courageous.[16] Eventually we habituate the rational soul to love those pursuits that are genuinely good and noble. This shows how it is in our original natures to develop a kind of 'second nature' of learned preferences and habits.[17]

Nicomachean Ethics, Book II focuses upon this trainable, emotive/desiderative part of the soul, describing what could be called the logic of right desire and correct choice attainable by the virtuously disposed soul. This turns out to be a kind of intermediate position between two opposite extremes. Here is how this works: virtuously disposed people desire the things that are genuinely worth desiring (as tending towards, or being constituents of *eudaimonia*) and are averse to those things genuinely harmful. But the right object – in order to count as genuinely good and fitting to the agent – must also be desired in the right way, to the right degree, at the right time, for the right reasons, and this implies an intermediate zone between excess and defect, between too strong or too weak a desire, between too little or too much of a particular kind of feeling or action.

Courage, for instance, lies somewhere between rash foolhardiness on the one hand and fear and flight from everything on the other. Generosity lies somewhere between being too stingy and being so liberal as to, say, impoverish one's family. A healthy diet, too, must be a balanced and adequate one, where this is determined by what would be too much and too little given the actual person in question. The virtues of desiring rightly are gradually developed, then, by the practice of abstaining from too much and too little.[18] Over time, natural but untamed desires will become stabilized into a rationally informed moderate disposition, a tendency that desires the mean, doing so with full awareness of the dangers to *eudaimonia* present at the other two extremes. Finally, when one habitually and spontaneously desires the mean between extremes, one has perfected (brought to maturity) the proper formation of the desiderative part of the soul: one has developed *moral* virtue (*ethike aretê*).

Of course, learning to feel and desire just the right balance of options between excess and defect, and to calibrate this accordingly as each circumstance may warrant, requires some sort of standard. This standard Aristotle provisionally calls 'right reason' (*orthos logos*).[19] Knowing just how to feel, choose, and act in a given situation will be something determined by the principle of right reason, and this is not a formula or quantity known in advance but is a principle that, at best, can only be stated generally. For the precise account of 'right' will depend upon the context and parameters of particular cases, and in these cases, the agents themselves must perceive and/or determine what is appropriate to the occasion.[20]

This intermediate state also includes an account of the pleasures and pains that accompany our apprehensions, desires, choices, and actions. For it is one thing to abstain from too much bodily delight and quite another to be pleased to do so. The vicious person may abstain, but inside he is pained by it; the temperate person abstains and delights in this. A character state can be judged by the things that give a person pleasure and pain, for someone with enough self-control can accomplish mere external action. Self-control alone, apart from taking delight in temperance itself, does not count as virtue.[21]

What kind of a psychological entity is moral virtue, then? To answer this question, Aristotle eliminates passions and the capacity to have passions: we do not praise or blame a mere capacity, and passions are context dependent for their evaluation. What is left is an acquired *state* (*hexis*) of character.[22] As with right desire, this state of character is described as a mean, an intermediate state between those tending towards excess and/or defect. As a *virtuous* state of character, it is a disposition that makes a person good and enables that person to perform well her own proper human function. It is a *state* that finds desirable and pleasing those things that truly are good for us as humans and which are, in fact, noble in their own right. It is, then, an acquired skill, a stabilized habit of choosing an appropriate mean, depending upon the context, of something conducive to one's own human flourishing.[23]

Choice, Freedom, and Deliberation

Because virtue is a character state that decides and chooses, Aristotle addresses two conditions upon which such a virtue must rest: volitional freedom, and the skill of sound deliberation. Both are necessary for a *eudaimonia*-promoting faculty of decision. Therefore, merely performing a just act, even taking pleasure in it, is still not enough. For to be truly just, one must perform the just deed under at least three further conditions: first, with full knowledge of what one is doing; second, having *chosen* to do it and chosen it for its own sake; and third, having acted this way from a stable and unchangeable character.[24]

Only voluntary actions are open to moral evaluation. Compulsive or ignorant actions, being motivated by principles external to the agent, are not considered praise or blameworthy. Not all forms of ignorance are to be excused, however, for an adult who is ignorant of the generally understood things that one 'ought to do' (e.g., one's children ought to be cared for) is a vicious person, whereas one who is ignorant of salient particulars in a moral situation (these are in fact *my* children) is not wicked, though perhaps that person should be pitied.[25]

Choice (*prohairesis*) is a species of voluntary action, and our choices reveal our character. But what is choice? Aristotle rejects certain candidates: choice is not an appetite or an emotion, neither is it an opinion nor simply a wish. These things may be related to choice but are not identical with it.[26] For us, choice must be of the humanly attainable; deliberation (*bouleusis*) must be of what is changeable through our choices.[27]

Since the ends of the good life, as we have seen, are based upon our human capacities and needs, both of which are given by nature, we deliberate not about ends but rather about the means of achieving them. The object of choice is that which is wished for in the deliberative process; once chosen, the object is desired in accordance with our deliberation. Hence, our choice or decision 'will be *deliberative desire* to do an action that is up to us.'[28] The definition of choice (*prohairesis*), then, is that it is a desire for some object that is now foremost among those having been deliberatively considered. Desire is for the end; deliberation and choice are of appropriate means.

In *Nicomachean Ethics*, Book III, Aristotle returns to an important theme – the phenomenological fact that whatever perceptual or noetic objects strike us prima facie as pleasant, noble, and desirable have in some way already been prejudged to be good and worthy of our love. If one loves horses, seeing a horse is somehow pleasant, and hence, greeted as a good thing to experience. If one loves violent crime, the sight of such things is also somehow pleasant and deemed some sort of good. Clearly, then, the state of character of a person predetermines (to some degree, at least) what things shall appear pleasant and what shall appear painful.[29]

Our tendency to perform what has been called an immediate 'perceptual judgment'[30] has two important characteristics: this desiderative-perceptual capacity is trainable; and this capacity does not by itself disclose the genuine good, only an *apparent* good. Consequently, moral judgment will require more than virtuous perception; it will lean on some *intellectual* excellence that co-produces, along with right desire, a correct answer to questions of deliberation. Book VI explores the intellectual virtues, in search of the best candidate for the rational side of deliberative desire. This candidate turns out to be *phronesis* – Aristotle's conception of practical wisdom.

Phronesis: *Practical Wisdom*

Nicomachean Ethics, Book VI examines the type of reasoning that pertains to deliberation and human action. If the choice is to be genuinely good, and choice is 'deliberative desire,' 'then the reasoning must be true and the desire correct.'[31] The good state regarding human action is not merely to know correctly, but to know a truth 'in harmony with right desire.'[32] After dismissing a few inappropriate candidates for what constitutes this 'good state' and qualifying others, it is *phronesis* that stands out as the intellectual skill required to form complete virtue.[33] But Aristotle does not treat *phronesis* as some abstract capacity that is best understood theoretically. Rather, he empirically investigates *phronesis* by considering the qualities of the person to whom it is attributed. We find that the *phronimos* is he who deliberates well concerning what is good and advantageous for himself, and not just in part, but over the whole of his life. Aristotle concludes that 'what remains, then, is that [*phronesis*] is a truthful habit of acting rationally in matters good and bad for human beings.'[34]

As such, *phronesis* is necessarily concerned with particulars, for all human action is concrete and particular.[35] Furthermore, practical wisdom regarding a person's choices and actions presupposes a layer of particular experiences through which practical insight is gained. Thus young persons, having little experience of the circumstances that life may present, find it easier to gain mathematical and geometric insights than practical ones.[36] No single, perceptual exposure to concrete particulars will produce practical wisdom, but repetitive perceptual and intellectual exposure may result in a cumulative set of exposures that, as a set, we would call 'life experience.' 'For it is length of time that gives *empeiria* – experience.'[37]

In the light of sufficient past experience, *phronesis* allows its practitioner to finalize deliberative inquiry through a kind of perception of the salient features within specific events and contexts. This is not, of course, by the intuition of any particular outer sense, but it is a kind of perceptual insight, since *phronesis* concerns concrete particulars, and these are things that are seen and experienced, unlike, say, the abstract objects of mathematics.[38] There is, then, a direct apprehension of some kind that is essential to the deliberations of the *phronimos.*

However, the ability of *phronesis* to grasp the genuine good end of human action distinguishes *phronesis* from mere shrewdness of calculation. Shrewdness, the art of a purely pragmatic calculus of means, cannot see the appropriate ends, for such vision is acquired by training and habituation in moral virtue. Therefore, it is impossible to have *phronesis* without also being good in one's desires and disposition.[39] Yet again, one could not develop right desires and an eye for the good and noble without having learned, to some degree at least, how to choose the intermediate between extremes spoken of above. It is also true, then, that no one can become virtuous without the deliberative savvy of *phronesis.* As Aristotle says, 'It is not possible to be good in the strict sense without practical wisdom, nor practically wise without moral virtue.'[40]

The ultimate purpose, then, of Aristotle's ethical writings is to help a student understand what it means to live well, to become good, to be happy in a fully human way over the course of one's whole life. The writings are offered to the kind of student who has already been put on the right track of virtue from her earlier years, having been raised in a context of good and noble pursuits and examples (say, among family and friends), and perhaps has lived under the pedagogical benefit of good laws and a just society. If in this way a student of virtue has already acquired, by habituation, knowledge of the things that are good and noble, then she is ready to embark on the path of the fully mature *phronimos.*[41]

For the key to complete virtue is not simply to know *that* courage, temperance, magnanimity, even temperedness, and justice are all excellences of the human soul, but to know that they are such *because* they really are good and noble in their own right, *because* they are genuinely choice-worthy for their own sakes, *because* they really are pleasant to embody as well as to behold, and *because* they really do make up vital aspects of a whole life well-lived.[42] Here we see an explicit ground of the objectivity of the human good in Aristotle's thought.

Indeed, the *phronimos* consistently chooses the good, but does so with full knowledge that X is chosen for its own intrinsic good and/or as an appropriate instrument to some intrinsic good. This is the kind of knowing not teachable in a classroom, but the kind acquired by personally experiencing the choice-worthiness of virtuous actions, by actually doing them and finding them pleasant to perform. This knowledge is, in the end, reflective. For having become virtuous, the *phronimos* experiences and understands 'from the inside,' both *that* he is doing well, and *why* this is so.[43] We can experience the freedom of pursuing our heart's desires, because these have now become shaped such that genuinely pleasant and wholesome things appear desirable while genuinely destructive things appear repugnant. Our desires are always for 'enough,' not too much or too little, of the many things that make up a human life. Thus, the mean has become attractive and we are able empirically to determine it with ease. Where complexity or newness of situation prevents us from immediate insight into the concrete good, we have become excellent at deliberating, in the light of a conception of whole-life flourishing, until we can finally 'see' what is to be done.

Thus, our desires are right and our reasoning reliable. If we are blessed enough to live in a time and place of sufficient prosperity and to have a social standing complete with honour and political enfranchisement, and to have these until the end, we are indeed flourishing in a quintessentially human way. We have *eudaimonia.*

Four Cognitive Operations Central to Aristotle's Theory of Moral Insight

In light of the above exposition, I wish now to draw attention to some key features of the perceptual and intellectual apparatus deployed by the *phronimos.* Later, I will compare these features to those in the cognitive theory of Bernard Lonergan. Lonergan has developed a detailed theory of the nature and operation of practical particularism (his 'common sense insight'), and I hope to show by comparison that Aristotle's ethical insight is a species of Lonergan's kind of particularist intelligence. It would follow, then, that Lonergan's notions of objectivity would apply to any particularist virtue ethic that works generally along Aristotelian lines.[44] That being my goal, I cannot in the scope of this chapter adequately treat all the pertinent issues and textual difficulties associated with perception and insight in the *Nicomachean Ethics* (or in *De Motu* or *De Anima,* for that matter). I will, however, develop the rest of my ideas here in the light of interpretations presented by Martha Nussbaum and Nancy Sherman, for their commentaries devote considerable discussion to phenomenological and cognitive factors in virtue-based ethics.[45]

Four relevant aspects of moral cognition derive from the foregoing synopsis and will be explored next. First, we will consider emotions and desires as cognitive or perceptive capacities. Second will be a study of *phantasm* – the phenomenal world of appearances, already shaped by our desires, and within which we must grasp the genuine human good. Third, we will examine a non-inferential mode of intelligence deployed within or towards appearances, namely, *phronesis*. Finally, there is that decisive moment during deliberation where some kind of direct intuition or perception determines a particular good relative to the agent (*aisthesis, nous, phronesis*).

Emotions and Desires

When speaking of emotion (*pathe*) I am not referring to bodily feelings (tiredness, hunger) or general moods with no intentional content (depression, irritability), but to the emotions such as fear, love, anger, joy, or disgust that accompany some object of thought or perception. These are the emotions that Aristotle classified as embodying a quasi-critical disposition of some kind; feelings that approve or disapprove, that attract or repulse, that evoke a desire to cling or to flee. Understood this way, emotions embody a certain kind of judgment,[46] and thus they seem able to interfere somehow with *rational* judgment, judgment *proper*. For impulsive desires and emotions may affirm illicit or inappropriate goals and objects, emotions may divert attention or distort the field to which we attend, and 'emotional' is a pejorative term used to describe persons whose characters are unpredictable or easily swayed. There is little doubt that emotions can be deceptive, or at least distracting, in the project of moral inquiry.

But in order to be able to deceive us, emotions must convey some cognitive content and not merely vague, non-intentional feeling. It is precisely this partly cognitive ability to sway us that reveals a power in emotions that may be put to good use: they may have a perceptive capability of their own and hence, present something to us for consideration; namely, a *value* of some kind.[47] For instance, my seeing an automobile and my liking it presents aesthetic and/or utilitarian value along with the purely rational content concerning the recognition and classification of the material object I am perceiving. Along with some sort of apprehension of value, there is apparently a concomitant prima facie judgment that the value is good or bad.[48] Thus, if my emotive response to the car is that I would never be seen in public driving it, my feelings convey the twofold content: 'aesthetic value is embodied here,'[49] plus 'this is bad aesthetics, i.e., ugly.' Such value-laden reactions are an 'interpretive seeing,' a kind of perceptual state much richer than simple registration of input and which is already a certain way of thinking about a given thing, though clearly a more instantaneous kind of thinking.

Much more can be said on this matter, but clearly Aristotle thinks that emotions augment our apprehension, enabling us to grasp value that is aesthetic, utilitarian, or ethical (good in itself). The *Rhetoric* showcases this succinctly.[50] That book is built upon an intentional theory of emotion, for the skilled orator is one who is able to evoke images and beliefs in the hearer that he knows full well will be responded to, quite predictably, with certain emotions. This would only be possible if emotion is in some degree open to cognitive input. Thus, an orator may present a jury with scenarios of injustice, evoking anger – not merely a nebulous annoyance, but an anger that is clearly directed towards the object it apprehends: the disvalue that is injustice. Fear and pity also take intentional objects and affect the way we perceive, as it were, the evaluative topography of some state of affairs. This gives emotion a vital part in our ability to discern good ends and appropriate means, and hence it is not surprising to find Aristotle including feelings along with the specific virtues and vices.[51]

It is clear, then, as we proceed to examine Aristotelian moral perception and deliberation that the phenomenal world we directly encounter, prior to any critical and dialectical interaction, is coloured by the current state of our likes and dislikes. These are reflected in our feelings and the value judgments implicit in them. Because our evaluative perspective is revealed by our construal of the world and our reaction to that construal, our emotions and preferences outline an ethical state description of our souls.[52]

Phantasm: *Appearances with Which* Nous *and* Phronesis *Must Work*[53]

For Aristotle, the capacity that forms a kind of middle ground between perception and thought, and which is fertile ground for emotional response, is *phantasia.* This capacity performs vital functions in aid of understanding, judging, and deciding. Aristotle's terms *phantasia* and *phantasm*, etymologically derived from *phainesthai* or *phantazesthai,* convey the notion of 'appearance' in the general sense, and that notion can be related to the terms as a capacity to experience appearances; the ongoing appearance itself; and that which appears as such.[54] At the outset of this discussion, the reader must understand that Aristotle is not limiting 'appearance' to only the visual modes of imagination and memory. Appearances may include presentations in consciousness involving all the sense modalities and in a variety of permutations. Thus, a remembered melody is an appearance, as are the meaningful tactile movements experienced by a touch typist.

Obvious evidence for an imaging capacity that is distinct from sensation is the experience of lingering impressions of things we initially perceived through sense perception. We have an object of sense, and then later on, through *phantasia,* we experience a re-presentation of that original sensation. As Brentano puts it, 'Whatever occurs in imagination was previously received in sensory perception,' and 'as an after-effect of sensory perception, imagination is weaker than the former.'[55] But this capacity does more than retain sense data.

If, according to Aristotle, the duration of each act of perception is limited to the presence of perceptible forms within the sense organ,[56] then some further capacity is involved in the apparent retention of sensations – a phenomenal continuance of formal impressions and their synthesis into larger wholes that form a 'field of vision' or a complex sense object enduring through time. For example, as we survey the details of a house, it is only discrete sections and elements that are informing our eyes at each moment as we sweep across the whole object, yet we retain somehow the appearance of the *whole house*, an 'overall impression' synthesized out of what we know to be discrete sensible moments. Such *phantasma*, while depending upon sense perceptions for their origins, take up a 'life of their own' in the form of complex after-images.[57]

Apart from such passive, synthetic usage, the terms *phantasm* and *phantasia* are sometimes more appropriately related to our capacity to deliberately evoke and creatively construct images; this is perhaps the dominant connotation of the English term 'imagination.' The term also, however, applies to the notion of 'mere' appearance (*phantom*) versus a 'real' appearance (*phainomenon*), linking appearances to discernment and judgment of some kind.[58]

In all cases, whether as retained sense information, synthetic and heuristic imagining, or mere appearances that temporarily bewilder the judgment, experiencing some appearance is a necessary condition for every type of thinking.[59] *Phantasia* plays an enabling role that bridges the gap between immediate sense perception and higher order thought – including ethical thought and practical deliberations.

Phantasia and the things it manifests, the *phantasmata*, serve functions beyond the perceptual level. They serve in discursive thinking about objects of sense.[60] They can also present objects that are not available to the senses at all, either because they are intellectual objects such as geometric concepts, or abstract objects such as the 'hollowness' of a 'snub-nose,' something understood through the images from which they are abstracted.[61]

But objects requiring 'ethical' insight are also *phantasm*-dependent. This is clear in Aristotle's claim that deliberation (*bouleusis*) and *phronesis* depend upon some capacity to imagine a *future* good state that is attainable by choice – future states being objects unavailable to the senses *proper*.[62] This would require an imaging capacity that links evaluation, knowledge, and appearances into some meaningful manifold, one that while beginning in sensations moves beyond them. As Frede puts it, 'All activities ... presuppose that I envisage something as good or bad for me, to be pursued or avoided. The necessary condition of my thinking that something is good or bad, according to Aristotle, is that the soul shall have certain *phantasmata*: I have to have the image of a future good or bad.'[63]

An operation that is at the same time both an act of reasoning and of imaging is seen in Aristotle's 'deliberative' *phantasia* (*phantasia bouleutike*). This is distinct from the basic perceptual imagination that we share with non-reasoning animals.[64] For it is on the level of appearances that reasoning animals consider whether to do one thing or another. This requires a calculation that is inseparable from what is presented, and to accomplish this, some type of rational comparison using images is being made. Thus, 'a reasoning animal is able to make one [*phantasma*] out of many *phantasmata*.'[65] H.S. Richardson says, 'This ... exhibits the intentionality built into *phantasia*, implying that a situation is seen in a certain way – as an appropriate time for rearing young, as a dangerous place to drink, etc.'[66] *Phantasia* itself is seen here to be discriminating and interpretive. Such deliberative imagination is the tool for resolving conflicts of desire. It allows for the combining and comparing of appearances in the deliberative process, for the measuring and comparing of relative goods and choices.[67] It seems, then, that the appearances of *phantasia* can themselves manifest a mode of deliberation.

Does this mean that *phantasma* must always be representative images, that is, pictorial-type presentations? For one of Aristotle's definitions of *phantasia* claims that its images ought to be 'similar' (*homoian*) to what they represent.[68] Must someone picture a snub-nose in order to abstract snubbedness, or can we think abstractions whose contents are extremely dissimilar to characteristics of the *phantasm*? Wedin and Nussbaum both agree that according to Aristotle, we cannot think in pure abstractions apart from some presentation – we cannot think of pure propositions or numbers.[69] Even if we were to think of, say, the principle of non-contradiction, we would need something like the image of a sentence or symbol that formulates the law or some instance of the law.[70] Linguistic and other symbolic tokens must be pictured somehow in order that we may think of contents that, in themselves, cannot be pictured at all.[71] And this allows Aristotelian ethics to refer to non-pictureable 'goods' such as *eudaimonia* – full flourishing over a whole life.

Furthermore, if *phantasma* must be of picture-like representations, then to perform the reasoning function just described, *phantasia* images must immediately convey what they are about. But one can inspect an image or scenario and fail to detect any definite 'aboutness' at all. An example seems to be Aristotle's own description of the parent debasing himself before the tyrant in order to ransom a captive child.[72] In that case, the image is exactly the same when at first one is pained by such an 'apparently' dishonourable action, and then afterward when one is more pleased to find out the parent is 'actually' engaging in an instrumental act for a greater good – rescue. In both cases, the 'pictorial content' of the presentation is the same, but it is additional 'descriptive content' that changes our understanding of what the scenario is actually 'about.' In fact, a mere pictorial presentation is not likely to have any definite semantic function unless it is embedded in some larger descriptive context.[73]

Now, combining this calculative, interpretive aspect of *phantasm* with a cognitive theory of emotion, we get what Aristotle clearly states: appearances are already partly shaped by our loves and goals. Our 'discriminatory activity is not, so to speak, prior to [our] response; it is in and constituted by [our] response [to appearances].'[74] The phenomenal world that we encounter, then, is not a world of brute sense data upon which thinking capacities go to work, but is a world already affected by subjective operations prior to our critical reflections. And this world is far richer than a series of pictures, but involves objects and beliefs that while dependent upon *phantasm* are themselves higher-order phenomena.

Martha Nussbaum has spent considerable time studying the role of *phantasm* in human thought and action. In her discussion of the cognitive nature of emotion and the fact that desire and aversion pre-construe the kind of appearances we face, she develops a richer conception of what 'interpretive seeing' will include. With the aid of this future-envisioning capacity and the memories and habits of past moral experience and learning, appearances can be as complex as *narratives.* This does not mean that we always need to tell ourselves little stories in which we then spot values. Rather, what we 'see,' though construed immediately by the expert eye of practical wisdom, still cannot be accounted for without recourse to a story-like description, and one possibly exemplifying many divergent, or even conflicting, human values. Surely some human goods cannot be pondered apart from a rather complex narrative that casts them in relief. This is presupposed by Aristotle's example just cited above, where a parent is seen groveling in self-abasement before a tyrant.[75] This is a scene that the reader greets with revulsion and disgust – until he discovers the larger context in which the parent is succumbing to blackmail in order to free a captive child. Aristotle uses a description that is designed to induce a kind of moral *Gestalt,* where an apparent evil suddenly snaps into an actual good, but only after the whole story is properly understood. While Aristotle offers this example during a discussion of what constitutes voluntary actions, it functions successfully as an instance of interpretive seeing precisely because in the dynamics of a story one can grasp values that are invisible in a state description alone. Nussbaum adds, 'If a general theoretical account [of ethical insight] is just what Aristotle is trying to undermine, then it would be in the spirit of his argument to turn for further illumination to complex examples, either from life or from literary texts. Like Alcibiades, he seems to support the *claim of concrete narratives to show the truth*' (italics mine).[76]

If deliberation involves understanding a complex circumstance in which past, present, and future actions may all become relevant, then narrative is really the only way to capture what lies beyond the scope of sensation and immediate emotive response to 'the way things stand.' Narrative enables us to replay a series of actions in our minds, and this certainly seems to be part of what deliberation requires. Thus, Nussbaum believes that exposure to good literature is an important part of moral pedagogy, for the good and noble in humankind is, perhaps, best seen in the concrete virtuous actions of ideal role models (say, the *phronimoi*). The poet, the novelist, and the historian all may serve a vital role in offering the 'appearances' that preserve and convey the noble deeds of the past for the pedagogical uses of the present.[77]

Nancy Sherman shares this view of *phantasma* as being, in many cases, as rich as narratives.[78] Though 'the stage of construal and discrimination needs to be distinguished from the moment of decision (or choice) in the light of the alternatives,'[79] still, both require a right construal of particular appearances. Affective responses (approval, hate, anger, disgust, horror, or pity) are not to actions per se, but to actions as responses to specific circumstances. Hence, to judge a particular case, we need to use *imagination* to recreate the *context* of the person we are judging. Story or narrative is required here – even an imaginary case perhaps – in order to judge rightly the ethical character at hand. Thus, the outside observer must judge from a virtual 'inside' supplied by imagination and the observer's own character.[80]

Finally, since we construe the world partly in accordance with desiderative tastes, and react orectically to that construed world, it is possible for those very reactions themselves to become the 'appearances' by which we can gain insight into the subjective conditions of our own moral characters. Sherman points out that when I reflect upon my *phantasm*-construal and how I respond emotionally, I discover that 'I am this sort of person,'[81] and I must manage the sort of person I am, shape myself, under some higher schema of good (*eudaimonia*). This reflective awareness comes from the phenomenological fact that the end appears to each person in correspondence with his or her character.[82] There is a reflective self-revelation that may ground the possibility of ongoing moral development, for it may reveal shortcomings, even shameful aspects of our character, that require our responsible attention. What we fail to see or are too afraid to face, the insights of a friend may provide.[83]

A full deliberation may include an assessment of one's own place within the moral narrative. The very term *bouleusis* connotes intersubjective counsel. Friendship may provide the discourse that leads to insights into the foibles of self as much as it may import an extra pair of eyes with which to scrutinize the circumstances.[84] There is, then, a collaborative element to moral perceptions, and not just during the pedagogy of one's youth but also for the mature person seeking to live well in the polis.

Up to this point, I have only touched upon some capacities of *phantasia* in order to show its vital role in practical thinking. Three of its aspects will be compared later to Lonergan's theory. First, there is the basic empirical world that presents itself to us with more content than can come from the sense data alone. We 'see' relations, apparent sizes, perspectives, optical illusions, but we also 'see' painful and pleasant objects and situations – and we see them *as* valuable (or not). The world comes to us already shaped, to some degree, by prior desires and beliefs – embodied in our emotional responses – but this is still properly spoken of as coming to us on the level of 'appearance' (Lonergan's 'level of experience'). Second, there is the fact that our imaging capacities are constantly in play in retaining stories that reveal or explain the ongoing phenomena of the world. Such narratives are vital aspects of moral discernment and deliberation, for they present to our mind's eye more than meets the physical eye. Finally, on the basis of *phantasmic* construal and emotive reaction, we are able to gain reflective insight, at least in part, into the subjective condition of our own characters.

On Non-Inferential Thinking

Next, we turn to the modes of intelligence that gain practical insight into the various permutations of *phantasm* just outlined. From the synopsis of the *Nicomachean Ethics* above, we already know some basic traits of *phronesis.* I want to enrich those descriptions somewhat in the light of the ideas of several of Aristotle's interpreters. The focus of this section is on the intuitive nature of the insights of *phronesis,* its reliance at some stage on deliberation upon direct perception of a concrete good. In a moment, I will look at the two difficult and related passages that speak of direct insight.[85]

We should recall that ethical ends are not acquired through deliberation, nor is there a demonstration that can deduce them. The deliberations of the *phronimos* are about *means* and not ends.[86] However, without an end in view, deliberation would never begin. Thus, some kind of apprehension of the final end of human action – living well, doing well – is necessary for the mature deliberations of the *phronimos.* And since living well is, in part, achieved through moral virtue, an apprehension of the elements of virtue is also required.

Initially, these must be received through sound moral teaching and instilling habits of acting and choosing. Thus, by repeatedly doing virtuous acts we learn experientially that courage, temperance, generosity, justice, and the like produce actions that are intrinsically pleasant and noble. We acquire the ends of ethical action first by faith, as it were, through sound teaching, and then eventually by direct personal experience of the worthwhile character of virtuous action. And so the first non-inferential mode of acquiring ethical knowledge, then, is by direct acquaintance with the intrinsic goodness of noble actions through becoming habituated to performing them, and eventually desiring them for their own sakes.[87]

But as we have just seen, such acquired desires shape our perceptions of the world. We encounter a phenomenal world that is already prejudged (to various degrees),[88] and it is to that world that we must attend in order to grasp ethical scenarios, objects, and narratives. Repeated exposure to and practical acquaintance (*aisthesis*) with appearances in this construed world gives us a foundation of experience (*empeiria*) that may sharpen our vision in spotting what is fitting in matters of practical choice.[89]

Before examining the non-inferential acquisition of ethical insight, we need to look quickly at the nature and role of education and social collaboration in the development of *phronesis.*

Acquiring ethical ends by faith, as it were, does not mean simply hearing ethical facts and arguments. Argument alone will not make someone good. Moral education is about instilling habits such that in their very performance the student would come to know the intrinsic goodness and pleasantness of virtuous action. Argument and fact knowledge cannot impart or remove habits. Still, some direct teaching of the means and ends to the good life can be taught by proposition, story, and example, provided that the student is already somewhat naturally endowed with a disposition to desire virtue and love the good, however undeveloped this may be at the outset.[90]

The imparting of habits of right desire to suitable students is effectively achieved in the collaborative and social contexts of mentorship, friendship, and good civil society. For the good person (the *phronimos*) will help his children and friends towards virtue.[91] When this is done in private life, there is the mentoring exemplified in parent–child relations and those friendships that are based upon good character. Regarding the household, the injunctions and habits of parents shape the child's preferences and habits, 'for the child starts with a natural affection and disposition to obey.'[92] By means of punishments and rewards (pains and pleasures), parents manipulate the choices of young children towards the genuine goods that will eventually be chosen and enjoyed for their own sakes when the child matures. Regarding friendship, among the benefits of good and virtuous friendship is the mutual learning and pleasure that comes when friends contemplate in each other the virtuous actions that each performs and that each would commend to the other.[93] Thus on a private level, as role model or friend, moral pedagogy proceeds more by spontaneous social collaboration than by some formal or written code.

However, when moral pedagogy is to happen on a more general and public level, the good person would teach by means of *legislating*, promoting the constraints and directives of good laws (or unwritten mores and customs) that would guide fellow citizens to behave in ways that, once habitually performed, would be desirable and useful for *eudaimonic* living.[94] Thus, the *phronimos* can be characterized as someone capable of sound legislation, both for herself and for her *polis*. Moral pedagogy is not, therefore, simply the imparting of a private intellectual skill at spotting right choices and objects. It is a social collaboration in which a taste for noble and virtuous actions is absorbed by the learner as one would acquire connoisseurship.

Let us return now to the analysis of *phronesis* itself. The practical perception of *phronesis* is not the operation of a distinct 'moral sense.' It is a discernment that operates in and through the normal senses.[95] This intuition should not be separated from other vital operations of the *phronimos*; namely, perception, reflection, and deliberation. These interact dialectically so that our perceptions and our deliberations mutually inform each other. For example, a situation may initially be construed as requiring courage. But this in turn may prompt us to reflect and reconsider, perhaps in light of other important values (e.g., a conviction of pacifism), until we come to understand a more nuanced view of what courage might finally require of us.[96] The perception-like grasp may come at the end of a far more complex process directed towards construed particulars. That is why Gomez-Lobo, for instance, says *phronesis* 'is operative when we perform well a *wide variety of interconnected intellectual operations* which aim at attaining truth in the domain of action' (italics mine).[97]

Aristotle gives a terse description of the process in the following example. I start with Sherman's translation of this difficult passage:

> Practical wisdom is obviously not scientific knowledge [*episteme*] for it is about the last term [*eschatou*] ... For the thing to be done is of this sort. And it is opposed to *nous*; for *nous* is about the first terms [*ton horon*] of which there is no account [*logos*], while practical reason is of the last things [*tou eschatou*], which is an object not of science but of perception [*aisthesis*]. This is not the perception of qualities peculiar to one sense, but of the kind by which we perceive that the last figure among mathematical figures is a triangle. For perception [*aisthesis*] will come to a halt here too.[98]

Practical wisdom here is seen deploying a process that terminates in a kind of perception. In Sherman's view, the problem being presented by Aristotle is one of how to determine the area of an octagonal figure.[99] The student may survey the whole figure, trying to dissect it into manageable parts so that area calculations could more easily be applied. After eyeing the form with different strategies in mind, wondering how best to approach the problem, the student suddenly realizes that the entire shape can be subdivided into triangles and – aha! – certainly knows how to determine *triangular* area. From here on the solution is academic. But recognizing shape is not merely categorizing what one instantly sees; it is discerning *how and/or why* the salient shape emerges from its interrelation to other shapes, and its place and role within the subsuming whole of which it is a relevant part. One sees the shape *as* a solution and not merely as a triangle. If this is what Aristotle has in mind, then he is arguing that practical wisdom 'requires seeing the salient "shapes" embedded in complex scenes in a way that enables an agent to make choices relevant to action.'[100]

In this regard, David Wiggins thinks *phronesis* begins with the agent's subjectivity – the idiosyncratic and prior set of concerns implicit in the question, 'What shall I do?' [101] This question prompts a series of operations: perception, imagination, inquiry, reflection, and the concerns and passions activated by thought experiment and high 'situational appreciation.' The geometer analogy just shows that in the question 'what should I do?' one seeks not a causal means; rather, one seeks a clearer specification of a more general concern raised by the circumstances. An individual desires to be, say, courageous, but must also know what would constitute courage in *this* particular circumstance. Only when one has grasped the best specification of courage in any given context does one have the goal towards which means-ends deliberations may apply.[102]

Since the competing claims of human concerns are not weighted and prioritized in advance, the deliberating subject is genuinely autonomous and may adjust the relative concerns in differing ways under differing contexts. This calls for a decision process able to account for redeployment of values and ideals in new situations, and generate a new understanding of old situations. Such a decision process would have to involve a dialectical dynamic by which unsatisfactory options may cause the agent to refer back to the original concerns and re-evaluate them in the light of the means available.[103]

In contrast to the geometer analogy passage, where *phronesis* grasps what is being sought, another passage by Aristotle claims that intuition of first principles is provided by *nous*. *Nous* has received various translations: 'understanding' (Irwin 1985), 'intelligence' (Rackham 1926), 'intuitive reason' (Ross 1930), 'comprehension' (Urmson 1988), and 'deductive reason' (Greenwood 1909). It is intelligence that can directly intuit its object, and in a later passage, *nous* does just this regarding practical matters:

> Now all action relates to the particular or the ultimate; for not only must the *phronimos* know particular facts, but understanding (*sunesis*) and judgment (*gnome*) are also concerned with things to be done (*ta prakta*), and these are ultimates. And *nous* is concerned with ultimates in both directions [i.e., with ultimates in two senses and respects, in respect of extreme generality and in respect of extreme specificity.] For *nous* [the general faculty] is of both the most primitive and the most ultimate terms where derivation or independent justification is impossible ... In its practical variety ... *nous* concerns the most particular and contingent and specific.[104]

Here, it is not *phronesis* but *nous* that does the direct grasping of practical things-to-be-done. Its perceptive power is discussed by Aristotle in *Nicomachean Ethics*, Book VI, chapter 8. There, he draws a contrast with chapter 6, where *nous* is the insight of non-demonstrable starting points (first principles) of all sciences (*episteme*). In practical matters, *nous* has a perceptual capacity for 'situation appreciation,'[105] by which the *phronimos* is directly able to 'select from the infinite features of a situation those features which bear upon the notion or ideal of human existence (*eudaimonia*).'[106] This is why each of the various translations of *nous* conveys the idea of 'seeing' as a metaphor for 'direct understanding or insight,' where 'direct' means a non-inferential, immediate grasp of ultimate particulars.

The geometer sees not merely *that* a triangle is a primary figure here but sees the triangle *as* a figure whose contribution to area calculation will, in fact, solve the whole problem. Thus, in the practical deliberations of the *phronimos*, the recognitional moment of Nussbaum's 'interpretive seeing' is accomplished by *nous* grasping an action precisely *as* a means to an end.[107]

Much more can be said, of course, regarding the various interrelated operations that the practically wise person deploys, especially in analysing the processes of deliberation (*bouleusis*), but my point is to show that *phronesis* amounts to a complex set of activities, for the one having it is good at a multitude of distinct cognitive and evaluative acts that terminate in concrete discernment, choice, and action. The cognitive operations of the *phronimos* begin, therefore, with perceptions aimed at a phenomenal world already construed in accordance with her prior character and end with a perception of the 'last thing,' an action to be taken, an insight that X is instrumental or constitutive of the desired end.

Though the final term of moral insight is a direct perception of some concrete thing-to-be-done, still Aristotle's use of a practical syllogism prevents us from leaving aside all reference to general rules of conduct and uses of inference.[108] Wiggins argues that in practice, the *phronimos* brings to bear upon the concrete situation the greatest number of pertinent concerns, and from this set of experiences, imaginings, questions, and thought experiments that reveal desires, there is grasped an answer to the question, 'What should I do?' – an answer that is specific to the circumstances and hence would form a *minor* premise in any syllogistic model of practical reasoning. Only now, when a minor premise is born from the particular context of the *phronimos*, is a major premise induced – one that illuminates the more general concerns embodied within specific decisions.[109]

Were it the case that courage, in fact, demands attacking the enemy immediately, there still needs to be a calculation of the best tactics, weapons, timing, and so forth. These final logistical considerations are also tasks for *phronesis.*[110] The fruit of *phronesis*, therefore, is its final practical judgment, made on the basis of intuitive perception (*nous*) of what the concrete circumstance requires.[111] For this to count as genuine *phronesis* and not mere shrewdness, however, the practical judgment must be made in the light of our general conception of the good life. This, as we have seen, is not an explicit reference to a philosophical worldview, but is a conception (of *eudaimonia*) implicit in the beliefs, emotions, and desires that construe the world for us.

The dialectic activity involving value-laden, construed perception and deliberative reasoning prevents Aristotle's *phronesis* from reducing to a simplistic grasp of a good 'out there to be seen' in the naturalistic sense. But it also stays clear of any strong notion of moral syllogism where general maxims exist apart from all reference to context and agent. The *phronimos* may make use of moral principles, but these do not function as universally binding maxims that *justify* our actions. Rather, as *post facto* generalizations of what might be morally relevant in a given case, general principles are to be understood as shorthand notes that summarize what has proven to be salient in countless past similar situations and therefore might be wise to consider in this case.[112]

We can see that Aristotle's perception analogy for *phronesis* is meant to show its partly non-inferential character. *Phronesis* is not a deductive science (*episteme*), whereby we derive correct choices from moral axioms. And it is not a *techne*, whereby direct application of general procedures of art will more or less guarantee correct outcome. *Phronesis* requires attentiveness to the actual circumstances impinging upon us, a calibration of decisions as the case may demand. This is what we do in navigation, medicine, and applications of the common law (e.g., *epieikeia*).[113]

Practical Particularism

Aristotle comes across, in Sherman's words, as a 'qualified particularist' who has a place for general but non-universal rules.[114] For Aristotle, choices are not subsumed under some general principle or law which itself grants the moral perspective. The 'mean' sought by *phronesis* is wise only if it hits the target in *this* case. It is not some constant moral injunction that one ought always to be moderate, for the mean might be an appropriate duration of extreme action or emotion. Rather, Aristotelian deliberation involves, in Nussbaum's words, a 'flexible movement back and forth between particular and general.'[115]

Even if we wanted to subsume a case under a universal moral maxim, precise understanding of the nuanced salience of each particular is required to make an accurate categorization. (This already involves a kind of evaluative perception prior to the rule.) For Aristotle, 'much of the achievement of moral practice is in the sorting out of the case itself.'[116] Again, we see that any schema of generalization comes after empirical expertise is accomplished.[117]

Finally, the justification for particularism involves at least these four major points. First, it is the particular perceptions, deliberations, and choices of the good person that set the standard. 'The good man [*spoudaios*] differs from others most by seeing the truth in the particulars, being as it were the norm and measure of them.'[118] *Phronimoi* and their perceptions are particulars. Second, regarding human action, statements concerning particulars are more trustworthy than statements about universals: 'For among statements about conduct, those which are general apply more widely, but those which are particular are more true, since conduct has to do with individual cases, and our statements must harmonize with the facts in these cases.'[119] Third, general moral principles are derived from the situational perception of particulars. For 'universals are reached from individual cases; of these, therefore, we must have perception (*aisthesis*).'[120] This was just stated above: particularist insights are a precondition of any ethical generalizations. Fourth, we can understand Aristotle's particularist approach by understanding his rejection of Plato's idea in *Nicomachean Ethics*, Book I, chapter 6. Rather than the Form of the Good being some unity in which all human choice and action must participate, the goods that constitute a flourishing human life are *plural.* Therefore, insight into particulars and morally salient features of concrete circumstance are vital parts of ethical judgment, for they are the only way to tell that we are collecting that plurality and harmonizing it appropriately to the ulterior end of *eudaimonia.* What gives a morally excellent choice its intrinsic value is not that it participates in an absolute Form of the Good, but that it is in fact choice-worthy for its own sake. It is choice-worthy because of its relation to us, to the kind of beings we are; it is genuinely good because it fits our humanness and aids in our flourishing, whether biological, emotional, intellectual, social, and so on. But the actual choice of the 'mean relative to us' will always be a mean relative to 'me' – the particular agent involved. Hence, the final choice requires a grasp of actual specifics.

Summary

This chapter has presented important elements of *Nicomachean Ethics*, Books I, II, III, and VI, and an exposition that isolated four distinct and interconnected cognitive operations vital to moral insight: (i) the power of emotions and desires to apprehend intelligible content, especially value; (ii) the construed world of appearances that emotions and desires play a role in forming and that they react to in proto-evaluative response; (iii) *phronesis* – that mode of practical intelligence (involving *nous*, *empeiria*, and *aisthesis*) that seeks to cope with concrete exigencies, doing so with the ulterior goal of *eudaimonia*; and (iv) the practical particularism that seems to follow from the nature of *phronesis*.

Emerging from this has been the problem of *phronimos*-as-subject; that is, how the personal experience, skill, emotion, and cognitive well-functioning of the agent has made more ambiguous our notion of 'being objective' in Aristotelian ethical insight. The problem is not one of whether Aristotle believed in objective moral truths, for he is explicit about this. There is truth in ethics, and that is why we must be concerned to distinguish between the apparent and the genuine. The genuine good is that which really would be good for us according to a correct understanding of human nature, and it is choice-worthy for that reason. The problem here is on the side of cognition: how is the activity of the *phronimos* said to be objective when relying upon apparently subjective or personal factors? How are we to think about the reliability of direct insight when contrasted, say, with deductive inference? Does not the developmental nature of moral expertise seem to indicate that the standard is a moving target, perhaps headed towards a convergence of moral truth, perhaps remaining socio-historically relative? Let me reiterate three main factors for wondering about just how the *phronimos* could be said to be objective in moral insight.

First, the *phronimos* uses her own contextually and historically conditioned disposition to somehow directly 'perceive' ethical salience within concrete circumstances, whereas within the same context the vicious agent is quite incapable of grasping the appropriate choices.[121] It is the past experience and right desire of the agent that induces awareness of salience. The agent, in making excellent ethical decisions, must not only come to know what is genuinely good to choose but must also desire it rightly, 'right desire' playing a role in both cognition of the good and in justification of a 'right' decision.[122]

Second, the object with which *phronesis* must interact is the world 'as it appears' to us. There is no other starting point. If, as we have seen, the states of affairs in which the questions for deliberation emerge are as complex as narratives, then interpretation of the narrative is vital to getting it right in moral insight. Yet narrative and its elements are already pre-interpreted (at least partially) by uncontrolled prior conditions in the subject before he confronts the phenomenal world. How are we to think about an objectivity that does not seek to overcome *phantasm* construal, since this is impossible, but seeks to achieve a 'right' *phantasm* construal?

Third, genuinely good choices are categorized as just those which are chosen by a rationale (*logos*) employed by a typical *phronimos.*[123] The good is just what the good person would choose. This raises the problem of apparent circularity in determining the good, and once again, the problem of how one is to 'be objective' arises.[124]

Since we do not seek to escape the contribution of the subject to the construal of the world and the selecting of salience, we need a notion of objectivity that does not function as some artificially external standard, but rather as an internal regulating notion, something that would keep the subject on track in her quest to live well. We need a subject-friendly model of objectivity.

2

Lonergan's Theory of Insight and Cognitive Operations

In pursuit of a deeper understanding of just which cognitive operations are at play when the *phronimos* gains moral insight, I turn now to the general theory of human understanding developed by Bernard Lonergan. We have seen how Aristotelian virtue ethics relies upon some mode of direct insight that grasps the human good within presented particulars, and it is precisely the vital role of insight that is richly explored in Lonergan's work.

Under scrutiny here are three major aspects of Lonergan's theory: the nature of insight and the overall cognitive process in which it plays the key role; the nature and role of a fundamental disposition of query that drives the whole dynamic of human learning and knowing; and the cognitive nature of human emotions. An overview of these elements will prepare us to move towards the development of a notion of moral objectivity that is based in a well-functioning human subjectivity.

The Nature of Insight

We begin by defining the term. Insight, as generally understood, is simply the mental event of 'coming to comprehend' something; it is not the *content* of what is understood, but the grasping of that content. 'To gain insight is to understand (something) more fully, to move from a state of relative confusion to one of comprehension ... [it] is associated with the "Aha!" experience, with the proverbial light bulb going on over one's head.'[1]

Though sometimes occurring instantly, insights can also occur in a series of unspectacular, gradual accumulations. They can occur within a broader set of operations, a family of phenomena occurring in creative work: 'the thesis, discovering similarities, analogies, increase in certainty, recognizing error ... and so on.'[2] Each of these stages in turn has an internal micro-genesis and occurs within a larger developmental sequence.

Insight can be triggered by memory and imagination as well as by perception. The history of science reveals amazing examples of insights occurring through the presentations of daydreaming states. Friedrich von Kekule's dream is a prime example.[3] These cases show the dependency of insight upon some mode of phenomenal presentation. It is not surprising, then, that studies of insight occurrence have shown a correlation between richness of memory, experience, imaginative ability, and success in gaining insight.

There are still other strategies that foster the inception of insight. These are attitudinal changes, and even environmental ones, that may increase the probability of hitting upon success. Schooler and others showed that the following techniques and attitudes often prove successful for overcoming an impasse:[4]

Forgetting. Allowing a passage of time to clear out useless routines and to de-emphasize the salience of inappropriate cues may be relevant.[5] The subject may, for example, decide to 'sleep on it' before making a final decision on an issue.

Changing context. Poincaré's flash of insight into Fuchsian functions occurred while on vacation.[6] Archimedes had an insight into the relation between specific gravity and water displacement while sinking into a bathtub in ancient Syracuse.[7]

Recognizing that one is lost. The subject moves back to a viewpoint where he can see the problem and his own inability to proceed. He can fail to recognize that he is in a rut or he can be too proud to face that possibility, thereby foreclosing the possibility of moving to more fertile problem space.

Perseverance. Despite the dangers of losing perspective or falling into a rut, there is an obvious relation between time devoted to a problem and probability of solution. This is true for experts as well as novices.

Risk taking. Big discoveries in science, for example, have often been long shots that required going out on a limb.[8]

Playfulness. Einstein referred to what he called the 'combinatory play' of selected ideas and representations, an essential feature of productive thought contributing to the process of insightful discovery.[9]

But most important is the ability to recognize *analogies.* As Schooler and others state: 'The value of analogy is that it may enable the individual to conceptualize better the ill-defined problem space in which he or she is working by relating it to some other problem space that is better defined.'[10]

These descriptions, based upon lab and field research, corroborate virtually all of Lonergan's earlier phenomenology of insight. He focuses on the nature of insight itself, but just as importantly, on the set of cognitive operations in which insight, when it occurs, is embedded.[11] Lonergan begins by noting that insight comes as a release to the tension of inquiry, and that it often comes suddenly and unexpectedly.[12] These characteristics are self-explanatory: an insight may instantly put an end to the tension of inquiry. But Lonergan goes on to observe that insight is not a function of outer circumstances but of inner conditions. By this he means that insight is not automatic, the way vision is if one merely opens one's eyes or the way hearing is if one is not deaf. To see and hear is automatic if 'outer conditions' permit; that is, if the light is strong enough and the sound waves have good amplitude. But the occurrence or induction of insights is a matter of statistical probability, and the conditions that increase the likelihood of such induction are such factors as balanced blood sugar, sufficient protein in one's diet, adequate sleep, alertness, depth and diversity of past experience, asking questions, special training and knowledge, creative visualization, living in a culture that supports and values discovery and free thinking, and so forth. All these factors are examples of 'inner' conditions that foster insight induction.

Lonergan states that insight pivots between the concrete and the abstract, meaning that insight is the link between sense and understanding; between presentation and implication; or, on a higher order, between 'knowing that' and 'knowing why.' It is by insight that we grasp, within concrete particulars and states of affairs, the characteristics on which will hang generalizations, analogies, taxonomies, and theoretic constructs. Clearly, this is the event that occurs in Aristotle's geometer example in the last chapter.

Some insights may become part of our habitual knowledge. Habitual knowledge denotes a set of accumulated insights that once acquired become the basis for increasing ease in learning and/or operating within a particular field. For insights do not accumulate in the linear and logical order of a flow chart or a deduction but amass themselves into clusters unified by sets of questions or concerns. Accumulated sets of insights form entire viewpoints from which we now easily grasp things that were a difficult mystery during the learning process. Accordingly, mathematics, analytic thinking, artistic style, tactics, and political savvy are all examples of clusters of insights that are habitually resident and operative in what we call expertise.[13]

Finally, accumulated insights of a lower order may be systematized by higher order insights. Algebra, for instance, involves insights that allow the intelligent manipulation of whole orders of lower arithmetic insights. Theoretical economics involves higher order insights that explain and systematize whole sets of lower order transactions. The plot of a novel systematizes what may otherwise seem to be inchoate actions and events in the narrative. Moving to such 'higher viewpoints' allows us to discover and integrate wholes and parts, events and recurrences, and to grasp the concrete historical development of systems of ideas and systems of techniques.[14]

Although I have described insight as the pivotal event of understanding, it is vital to stress here that insight occurs as the key element in an overarching, dynamic set of operations that, taken as a whole, makes up Lonergan's 'generalized empirical method'[15] and which may be referred to as our process of 'coming to know.'[16] I will explore this larger set of operations within this chapter, but here it is important to understand that while an insight itself is the breakthrough we seek in our desire to know things, any particular insight is not a fully epistemic state itself: it embodies content and may also provoke the psychological 'aha!' response, but it is not yet a justified belief. The process of coming to know is an ongoing, self-criticizing and self-correcting procedure. The process may eventually issue in truthful propositions, but these will not simply jump out as obvious to us but will be affirmed by critical grasp of sufficient reasons for assent, whatever those may be. Thus as we proceed in this study, while the context will occasionally allow me to use the term 'insight' to refer to the whole process of coming to know, properly speaking, the two must be distinguished.

Human knowing, according to Lonergan, is discursive, involving different levels of cognitive activity: attention, perception, memory and imagination, insights, formulation of these into concepts and definitions, reflection upon these, conjecture, weighing and considering evidence, judgment – and following upon all of these, decisions, choices, and actions. Insight is the hinge that links the inquiring subject from one distinct kind of cognitive activity, say perception, to the next, say hypothesizing. As such, it makes the difference between an animal's gawk and a human's understanding. Thus, we seek insights for what they provide to the whole generalized empirical method of 'coming to know.'

With this caveat in place, I wish to illustrate this methodical cognitive activity at work by turning to the remarkable case of Helen Keller, a woman whose insights were gained through tactile data only.[17] As a child who became deaf, blind, and mute, Keller lived within a world of immediacy limited to the sensations of touch, taste, and smell. Her special-needs teacher understood that Keller could only escape the limitations of her world by shifting her focus from rudimentary sensation to the semiotic realm of mediating signs. So with her finger, she began inscribing the letter 'W' upon the palm of Keller's hand while holding it under running water in the hope that Keller would associate the tactile letter with the water. The success of this technique changed her life. Writing about this event much later on, Keller said that when she suddenly grasped that link – of 'W' to water – it was as though the heavens had opened and she was flooded with light. She got the point! She gained insight into the curious sensible phenomenon of scribbling upon her hand, but to make absolutely sure of her discovery, or rather her hypothesis, she grabbed a handful of dirt and offered it to her teacher. When she then felt a different letter, the letter 'E' (for earth) being inscribed, she affirmed the correlation of the sign and the signified. This was not an insight into water or earth; it was insight into the notion of a sign, a language – and it lifted her from a world of introversion and crude understanding to one of higher meaning and self-expression.[18]

The Complex Cognitive Process in Which Insight Operates

The example of Helen Keller highlights three interlinked cognitive operations which, when operating without obstruction, form our process of coming to know; that is, Lonergan's generalized empirical method. First there is inquisitively directed *attention* to the data of presentation;[19] second, the occurrence of insights of *understanding*; and third, the reflective insights of *judgment*. A final level of apprehension that may follow is the insight and judgments of *value*, conveying what would be genuinely worth pursuing in human action. Let me give a cursory description of these related operations.

The first level of our method of coming to know is an inquisitive attending to some phenomenal presentation. There is a flow of intentional data, including the presentations of memory and imagination, which impinge upon consciousness. The first act of intelligence is to direct interested attention upon some part of the flow and prescind from others; such attending has a heuristic focus absent from, say, daydreaming. Attending is not itself an act of sense, but is a shift in intentional focus directed, according to Lonergan, by the subject's own concerns, wants, needs, and so on. Attention is not random, though it is often spontaneous; it is an intelligent dividing of the flow of consciousness into meaningful and manageable parts. For Keller, this was to focus on the tactile experience of scribbling upon her hand, rather than, say, the coldness of the water; but there are many ways to attend. Our attending can be a very light bemusement with some presentation; it can be seized and jolted in a new direction by sudden interference; it can be fascinated with a clue implying some larger mystery; it can be a plodding and deliberate concentration on the necessary task at hand. In all cases, attending is intentional and its object is some presentation, some data in conscious awareness.[20]

By means of the objects of attention, there may be induced the second-level cognitive event of understanding. This is experienced as the occurrence of an insight, whether climactic 'aha!' or gradual dawning. Insights of understanding grasp the intelligibility immanent within experienced data or that may apply to these data. Merely to understand something pertaining to attendant data is to have an insight into *possible* meanings or links, a grasp of some coherent formal content, a grasp of the distinction between the essential and the accidental within the focused data. In Keller's case, this was the grasp of the possibility of a relation between the scribbling and the water. Such insights of understanding are the links that shift us from mere experience to intelligible grasp, but they are still, in fact, hypothetical until reasons for assent obtain. But affirmation and denial are themselves the result of a further insight: the reflective insight of judgment.

At Lonergan's third level of cognition, we use judgment to discern the actual from the possible, the real from the merely apparent. This query calls for the higher order insight of critical reflection that verifies, denies, assigns a probability to, or seeks further evidence for the initial insight of understanding. The insight of judgment results in an assent; thus it is not an act of will, a decision, but an act of intelligent apprehension that fulfilled conditions compel affirmation. Keller's first insight was something like, 'Aha, "W" *means* water!' This is what she thinks, but how can she know that such an assertion is true rather than just a 'bright idea?' Her move was to formulate the content within a conditional and then seek fulfilling conditions; for example, 'If other tactile objects have distinct letter-signs, then "W" must apply uniquely to water.' The conditions were fulfilled by a turn to *phantasm* (tactile), where she felt 'E' for earth being scribbled on her palm while holding some soil, and thus she confirmed both that such scribbles were signs, and that 'W' meant water. The insight of judgment, then, does not grasp a further content (say, truth or being) within the first order insight; rather, it reflects upon the *link* between a conditional and its conditions, and grasps the presence of fulfilled conditions sufficient for assent.[21] This constitutes the third essential level of cognition in Lonergan's 'dynamic process of knowing.' It is here on the level of judgment that the whole process attains to what we call knowledge *proper*. The insight of judgment completes the process by ending the query in a true epistemological state: Keller now *knows* that 'W' means water.

Both the insight of understanding and the insight of judgment are the same kind of cognitive event, a grasping of something by turning to conscious presentation. Both may or may not be accompanied by the psychological 'aha!' experience. What distinguishes them is their formal intentional object; understanding grasps a form, a *what* it is. This can be a simple essence or definition, or it can be a complex concrete state of affairs. But judgment asserts or denies being or truth, not form. On the one hand, then, insights of understanding answer to questions that seek the *what* and *why* pertaining to conscious presentation. On the other hand, insights of judgment result from reflection upon insights of understanding. They seek to know whether what is understood is indeed the case – whether 'W' *really does* mean water. I will offer more discussion of this later on.

This ongoing cycle – attending to presentation, insights of understanding, and insights of judgment – forms the basic structure of our dynamic process of coming to know. Since our inquiry is concerned with human intelligence as it would unfold within *ethical* inquiry, however, we must consider not only the above three operations, but also whatever insights might be involved in deliberating and deciding. Such insights would result from their own line of query typified by such questions as the following: What should I do? Should I in fact do it? Would doing this be genuinely worthwhile? These and similar questions will involve another distinct kind of insight that for Lonergan would include some turn to emotion and desire as well as to *phantasm.* This type of insight he classified generally as an 'insight of value.'[22]

A fourth level of operation may therefore also occur, consisting of insights and judgments of value. The above deliberative questions involving value assume a level of self-awareness where one moves to a higher viewpoint that considers the self within the larger contexts of one's past, one's social embeddedness, and one's beliefs and desires, including what kind of person one desires to become precisely through one's own deliberations and decisions. From this higher viewpoint, we may ask the questions for deliberation and decision that take into account longer-term concerns and life goals. Accordingly, deliberative insights present future possibilities; judgment affirms that striving for these possibilities is truly worthwhile. Clearly, this is the line of questioning and insight within which much of practical ethics takes place.

This whole process of attention, insight, and judgment – and in the case of practical and ethical knowledge, deliberation and decision – cycles through itself in a self-correcting spiral of learning.[23] It is self-*correcting* because any formulated insights and judgments always remain open to further questioning: Are there more relevant data? Are there more relevant implications? Is this really the case? These questions and their answers may lead to actions, observations, experiments, new insights, and re-formulations that in turn become the data upon which the process will begin all over again. It is *self*-correcting because the same process will detect any failures or inadequacies, for correction can only come by further attention, insight, and judgment. Thus it is the one process, reduplicated back upon itself, that effects self-correction and spirals towards the ongoing development of our various blocks of knowledge.

Finally, this process, while *spontaneously operative* in the development of human thought, may be responsibly and methodically harnessed. The successive stages usually are not explicitly conscious to us, often awaiting some frustration of our inquiry before becoming obvious. Yet though we experience the process as spontaneously operative, it is quite possible to appropriate it and deliberately, self-reflexively operate according to its exigencies. This is what empirical science has formalized: the methodical exploitation of cognitive processes already at play. (The first three levels of the cognitive process correspond to empirical, hypothetical, and verification procedures.) Moreover, we may find ourselves very deliberately appropriating the stages outlined above whenever we seek to reaffirm or question a conclusion. For we find ourselves carefully and consciously reiterating the stages of attending, comprehending, and affirming (or denying), and we seem to have an immediate sense that error is found only at one or more of these levels if something proper to each level has failed to obtain. Thus, by taking a spontaneously functioning set of operations and deliberately and self-consciously deploying it, we take a native dynamism of human cognition and transform it into a method. It is a method productive of beliefs that can be justified and known to be true.[24]

Wherever we have a method that can be deferred to at will, we also have an operation available for responsible use or thoughtless misuse. In anticipation of later chapters, let me state here that by describing human knowing as a set of mental acts that we may harness, perfect, or disregard altogether, Lonergan sets up cognitive process as an issue central to any virtue ethics. For his cognitive process is open to being developed (or not) into a well-functioning habitual structure or suppressed by a willful flight from insight. We are, therefore, vulnerable to praise or blame for what we do in this regard. Insofar as the subject is self-aware and responsible in the deployment of cognitive method, the subject is performing an essential function of the *phronimos*, an excellence in seeking to know – one case of which is deliberation.[25]

The Unrestricted Nature of Questioning and the 'Pure Desire to Know'

The foregoing modes of being conscious – as attending, as understanding, as reflecting and judging, deliberating and the like – are all manifestations of a prior disposition that elicits these conscious acts in the first place: the disposition of query, wonder, curiosity, or personal concern. We may experience a dissatisfaction with *not* apprehending, *not* understanding, *not* knowing what is true and what is good, and this dissatisfaction motivates further inquiry (in the well-functioning, authentic subject).

For this reason, Lonergan regards the process of coming to know as fundamentally heuristic rather than intuitive. While some stages in the process involve direct apprehension of content (attention to conscious presentations), the process itself is driven by an intending aimed at a content we do *not* yet know. This intending of the unknown is exhaustive, for we can wonder about the things that we do not yet know, and we can wonder about all the remaining things that we do not even know that we do not know. This leaves out nothing. Thus, we can add a further point to Aristotle's principle that 'the kinds of things we can know are determined by the kinds of questions we can ask,'[26] which is that there is no restriction whatsoever to the kinds of things we can ask about. The process of coming to know is driven by query, and there is no a priori limitation to where questions can be directed, for there is no limit to what we can wonder about.

This bears repeating. Could there exist a kind of being about which *even to wonder* is impossible? Let us call this being an 'epistemological black hole,' for it provides no intelligibility at all to any observer or thinker. Now, either it will have a nature of some kind or it will not. If it has a nature, but one which is in principle cut off from my ability to discover, am I not still able to wonder about it? Am I not intending that nature as 'that which I would love to know, if only such a being were open to my cognitive capacities?' Thus, I am wondering about this kind of being – what it is, whether it is. But if the being has no nature all, then there is no formal content to be grasped by insight and affirmed in judgment, and hence I am wondering about nothing, and nothing does not count as a mode of being about which I cannot even wonder. Thus, simply to ask this question – is there any being about which I cannot even wonder? – is already to have a negative answer, for I am wondering about it by asking this question. Clearly there are practical limits to what humans will come to know, but the unrestricted nature of query is one of the prior conditions for the possibility of attaining genuine knowledge of the universe.[27]

Moreover, the intending of query cannot ultimately be satisfied until we know everything about everything. For while there are practical limits to what we will in fact wonder about, and the human lifespan is one of those limits, in principle we can always keep on wondering as long as things still perplex us. Thus, human query is ordered towards its own resolution in absolute knowledge, though clearly no one attains that. This is why Lonergan describes the query-driven process of coming to know as heading towards an ideal limit of 'no further questions.'[28] Lonergan argues that though each level of the process intends its own formal object, the whole process itself embodies an open-ended intending of 'all that can be known' by questioning.[29]

Let us turn to the a priori ground of questioning to study its role in the cognitive process: the 'pure desire to know.' Wonder, query, piqued interest, the concern to know – whatever we call it – is a primordial thrust towards being that is immanent in human consciousness. This eros of the mind Lonergan calls the 'pure desire to know.'[30] He is not speaking of a surface curiosity that makes us look up something in a dictionary, for example. Rather, it is that thrust that would raise a question in the first place. It is revealed in the very propensity to be intrigued by pattern, salience, or change within *phantasm.* It is felt as a dissatisfied ignorance, an annoyance with error and the turn to seek correction. Lonergan describes it this way:

> This primordial drive, then, is the pure question. It is prior to any insights, any concepts, any words; for insight, concepts, words have to do with answers, and before we *look* for answers we *want* them; such wanting is the pure question.
>
> On the other hand, though the pure question is prior to insights, concepts and words, it presupposes experiences and images. Just as insight is *into* the concretely given or imagined, so the pure question is *about* the concretely given or imagined. It is the wonder which Aristotle claimed to be the beginning of all science and philosophy. (italics mine)[31]

As a desire, the pure desire to know seeks fulfillment in the satisfaction of acts of knowing. But as a desire to *know,* it does not simply seek the satisfaction that cognition may give the subject, but desires the *content* of cognitive acts. Such a desire is limited only by 'what there is to be known'; that is, the totality of intelligible reality. As we have just seen, the pure desire to know can only be satisfied when we know everything about everything, though in practice, in a given context it ceases when we know that no further relevant questions will arise. For example, it is hard to imagine any real questions that would resurrect Ptolemaic astronomy; that system stands defeated by the answers given to a completed set of questions.

It is the pure desire to know that arranges the levels of cognitive operation into a hierarchy of functional dependence: data invite questions for understanding (what is it?), and these may yield insights (according to some statistical rate); but insights themselves raise questions of judgment or verification (is it indeed so?) of whatever content is conveyed in the first insight. Based in part on what we affirm as real, we respond affectively and responsibly, with questions of deliberation and decision (what should I do? how should I live?).

This hierarchy of dependence grounds a normative method.[32] Doing things in this order is the right way of going about the process of coming to know. Failure can occur in several ways. There is the failure to allow any level to reach its proper term. Thus on the level of experiencing the data of presentation, we may fail to be attentive, daydreaming instead of concentrating, being waylaid by trivial detail and missing salience. On the level of inquiring intelligence, we can fail to let insights fully emerge or fail to allow several contrary insights to coordinate themselves vis-à-vis the same data.

We can fail by refusing even to entertain certain insights because they violate a preciously held bias or dogma. On the level of reasonable and critical reflection, judgment may become rash and affirm an insight despite insufficient reason, or it may refrain from affirming an insight even in the face of evidence because of fear or dislike of the conclusion. In all cases, it is the prior pure desire to know that elicits query in the first place that is now prevented from driving the process, and the natural cycling of attention, insight, and judgment is curtailed by some unhealthy interference.

We can more easily conceive the normative aspect of the pure desire to know through such a negative analysis. For the pure desire to know is that primordial thrust that is stymied by inattentiveness, bias and repression, rashness and cowardice of judgment, and vice in deliberation and decision. Something has broken down when any or all of these pathologies are in play, and that something is a dynamism that was heading towards the real, the true, and the good before it was waylaid by defects in the operations of human subjects. In Lonergan's theory, the inhibition of the pure desire to know, and hence of the cognitive operations propelled by it, is a fundamental cause of our failing to attain objectivity in our knowing process.[33] I will return to this in later chapters via an analysis of the problem of bias.

Because the ordered operations are all conscious, they can be *known* to be the norms that functionally they are. This can be phrased in hypothetical imperative language: if your fundamental desire is for an intelligent and reasonable grasp of reality, then pay attention to the data, gain insight, judge validly, and decide in the light of these.[34] The order of dependence of the operations, then, is normative, as is the thrust to perform them; it is the 'right way' of going about knowing. Any deviation from this order results in a procedural error.

Lonergan's argument is that this pattern of linked cognitive operations is normative and foundational for all our other, more specific heuristic methods, such as modern science. For any specific project of human knowing, such as science or history or moral inquiry, will employ its own more determinate modes of attending, insight induction, and critical reflective judgment. And the generalized empirical method, as an immanently operative norm grounding these projects, will also ground the objectivity proper to all sub-species of human inquiry.

Two Cognitive Roles for Emotion

In his later work *Method in Theology*, Lonergan begins to explore the cognitive role that emotions might play in our process of coming to know. His general conclusion is that emotions apprehend *value*.

After distinguishing somatic sensations (hunger, fatigue) and general moods (depression, irritability) from feelings as responses to intentional objects (anger, fear, joy, grief, compassion), Lonergan claims that such intentional responses are the very apprehension of things deemed valuable to us. To understand what he is getting at, we need to distinguish two basic cognitive roles played by intentional-response feelings – as apprehensions of value and as determiners of our horizon of concern – and then contrast those roles with the judgment of value proper. First, feelings are apprehensions of value. Lonergan discusses two types of feelings: responses to intentional objects that are deemed satisfying or dissatisfying, and responses to intentional objects deemed values in themselves.[35] In the first case, feelings respond to an object with pursuit or avoidance because of its relation to the current desiderative state of the subject. In the second, feelings are responses to objects for the sake of which the subject is willing to gain new desires or eschew presently inappropriate ones. The first is simply the emotional response to things we happen to like or dislike, prefer or reject (apart from any real good they may embody). The second is the emotive recognition of some object or action that is seen as an intrinsic good, whether or not we have yet established a habit of preference for it. It is this second, intentional response that Lonergan calls the apprehension of value, as opposed to the first, which is the apprehension of possible satisfaction. Through the apprehension of value, emotion selects or is attracted by an object for the sake of which we are willing to transcend the self that we are, to become something we are not yet (e.g., virtuous.) The apprehension of value, then, is a vital component of the possibility of moral growth.

Lonergan's treatment of satisfaction-feelings versus evaluative-feelings seems to parallel Aristotle's treatment of the merely pleasant versus the genuine good.[36] We feel positive emotion towards the things we happen to prefer and that give us the pleasantness of satisfaction, but neither preference nor satisfaction are indications that the object is genuinely good for us. For Lonergan as for Aristotle, the goal of desiderative, ethical growth is to move from a fundamental orientation of satisfaction-seeking to one of genuine value-seeking, and presumably this will yield its own higher kind of satisfaction. It is an excellence in our desiring faculty as well as one in our deliberating and practical reasoning that accomplishes this.

The first role of intentional-response emotions, then, is that through their proper orientation we may apprehend value. Second is the cognitive contribution of emotion as it establishes our horizon of concern. What is this horizon? 'Literally, a horizon is a maximum field of vision from a determinate standpoint. In a generalized sense, a horizon is specified by two poles, one objective and the other subjective, with each pole conditioning the other.'[37] The horizon of concern is the maximum threshold of the possibility of personal interest in some matter of fact or value. It is the limit beyond which we would not even know that we should care or inquire. And it is set, in large part, by a subject's emotions.

The analogy of three concentric epistemological circles may help us understand the concept: the innermost circle represents the things that we know, the next concentric circle represents the things we know that we do not know, and the outermost circle represents the things that we do not even know that we do not know. Within the first circle, I can wonder about and care about things; I can ask question and get answers; I can have concerns and know how to deal with them. Within the second circle, however, I may wonder and care about things that I know I do not know, and for that very reason I am driven on to learn and discover the things that are of concern to me. But regarding the outermost circle of the *unknown* unknown, I do not even ask questions nor do I care at all. The unknown unknown may certainly be intelligible and valuable in itself, but for me, it is beyond my world of cognition and concern.[38] Our personal cognitive horizon is the boundary between the second and third circle, between the known unknown and the unknown unknown. Our cognitive horizon is the limit beyond which we have absolutely no knowledge and no concern whatsoever.[39] Clearly, this boundary will have ramifications for a theory of objectivity.

As with knowledge, so with human concern: there is the circle of active cares, there is the circle of things I am concerned to develop suitable cares about, and there is the circle of that to which I am affectively oblivious. Now it is emotion that plays a vital role in the establishment of this horizon. The things about which I feel absolutely nothing will fall outside my horizon of concern and have no bearing upon my goals and deliberations. If there are genuine human goods beyond my horizon they will be cut off from my consideration, and to that degree my moral growth will be hindered. These things will not enter into my deliberations nor bother my conscience. (And I would not know this, nor care.) For example, if I keep the subjective suffering of non-human sentient animals in the third sphere of non-concern, this will affect the ethical decisions I am able to reach even through the most pristine deliberative process. Feelings establish the horizon within which deliberation takes place, for the things we will deliberate about will first have to be included within the horizon of things we care about.

But this raises an interesting point. Once we become aware of the third of the concentric circles, the one that precludes our possible concerns because of the limitations of horizon, we may become aware that ignorance of the real and the good is a matter for personal concern (for what I do not know *can* hurt me). Thus the pure desire to know, if left to its own exigency, should naturally push our horizon outwards towards the ideal limit of 'no further relevant concerns.' In matters of value and the good, it is the emotion of a disquieted conscience that drives this process, for a peaceful conscience is just another term for 'no further relevant questions.'[40] Thus it is through feeling that I apprehend the value of a maximally expanding horizon; I am made uneasy by knowing that a horizon is not itself an end to questions, but a limit to what I know how to ask.

Feelings, then, in Lonergan's schema, do at least two things. First, they are the very medium in which concrete personal value is initially apprehended. Second, they establish the limits of what we will be concerned about in the first place, and yet they may motivate us towards an unhindered expansion of horizon or towards inhibition of such openness through bias or repression.

With this twofold role for emotion in mind, we turn to the judgment of value. For Lonergan, because the human good is always *in* things, the judgment of value concerns the concrete and the particular. Like judgments of fact, value judgments are assents to insights based upon the grasp of sufficient fulfilling conditions. This is a very important notion that requires a moment's careful attention.

Generally, judgment has been used to name two distinct mental acts: composition and division (synthesis and analysis); and the positing or rejecting of whatever is understood in composition and division. The act of composition and division is part of the induction process of first order insights of understanding. We analyse in order to comprehend parts and relations: disassembling a motor teaches the apprentice how it works. We predicate attributes and relations of something in order to understand *what* it is: this motor is broken and belongs to Mr Jones. But whatever we come to understand through such composition and division (whether conceptual or practical) may still be subject to acceptance or rejection. It occurs to us that 'Aha – Jones's motor is broken'; but we may still reflect upon that insight and ask, 'Wait a minute, is it *really* the case that Jones's motor is broken?' It is this second question that indicates Lonergan's notion of judgment, the 'yes' or 'no' directed towards some proposition.[41] A judgment is always an answer to a question of the general form, 'Is it indeed so?'

However, one cannot move directly from a question such as 'Is it so?' to an answer. No matter how quickly we seem to make judgments, there is no direct intuiting of the 'yes' or the 'no.' There must be at least one stage, sometimes unconscious to us, between the question and the answer.[42] Lonergan claims that this stage is the formulation of the insightful content into a *conditional*, a hypothetical content. This can be done in any number of ways and relies upon learning, aptitude, creativity, skill, and other inner conditions. For instance, by adverting to the sensible presentation coming from the corner of my eye, I grasp that my daughter is coming down the sidewalk towards me. But realizing that school is not out yet, I question whether indeed that is my daughter coming towards me. Remembering that she wore a jean skirt this morning, I formulate, either explicitly or semi-consciously, the conditional: 'If upon closer inspection the clothes are the same, then my daughter is indeed heading this way and (aha! – a further insight) school must have ended early today.' Now all that remains is ascertaining whether the conditions have been met. If so, I have reason for assent. And if no further relevant questions arise, my attention shifts elsewhere. Judgment, then, consists in the coming together of two things: a conditional and its fulfilled conditions.[43]

But when we turn to ethical judgments of value rather than judgments of fact, we are concerned with *future* being, with what *should* be, not with what already is, and therefore present states of affairs cannot supply data sufficient to fulfill conditions. It seems, then, that an ethical value judgment will have to rely upon the sheer invulnerability of the insight to critical reflection. Desire, emotion, and insight combine to present us with some value-laden object of choice. The process of evaluative judgment seems to be a kind of process of elimination as our verification procedure seeks to remove doubts about our feelings and objects of desire: 'Is this indeed an intrinsic value I am pursuing or a veiled special interest of mine? Have I really paid attention to all the pertinent points of view on this matter? Am I repressing important feelings that need to emerge in this case?' In other words, we return to the steps of cognitive method and to the data conveyed in emotion and desire in order to come to a final judgment. We assent in a judgment of value when we no longer find reasons *not* to pursue what desire and/or emotion have presented to us in insight. I think this is the best way to interpret Lonergan's 'invulnerable insight' criterion.[44]

Clearly, then, judgments of value will not have the precision of judgments of fact or deductive method. For due to the inherent limits of any individual horizon at any one time, there is no guarantee that relevant questions will be asked or be recognized as relevant. The more sensitive, open-minded, and experienced a person is, the more likely she is to raise and answer the more relevant questions. Thus the process of insight and judgment of value is amenable to development, progress, and expertise.

Once again, it is by the criterion of 'no further relevant questions' combined with feelings that apprehend values that we make judgments of value. We feel the value of nobility, generosity, courage, and love, and we judge, by a competent set of past insights, that such and such a circumstance would be an appropriate manifestation of these values. It is not merely that we turn to judgments of value to decide the best instrumental means for a desired outcome, but that the judgment of value is the recognition that a particular concrete state of affairs is desirable because it would manifest a value that we first apprehend in feeling. If our conscience throws up no questions, we decide that we *may* proceed, not that we *must*, for the judgment of value permits; it does not command.[45]

This leaves much unsaid. For now, I have attempted to distinguish the *apprehension* of value in emotions from the *judgment* of value that is still an intellectual operation, but one dependent upon emotion for some of its material. This distinction will be relevant to my later critique of Nussbaum on value judgment. Here, however, I have wished also to show that value judgment is just as much a matter of the pure desire to know being allowed to operate without emotional baggage, so to speak. For just as emotion can shift appropriately our horizon of concern, unhealthy emotion can freeze it in place or shrink it, repressing relevant feelings and questions because these threaten a cherished bias or a comfortable status quo.

Summary and Critique of Lonergan's Theory

This chapter has introduced the reader to some major themes in Bernard Lonergan's theory of human understanding, in which he presents human knowing as a process that involves empirical, conceptual, and syllogistic components. If we chart the development of human knowing from the inception of an attitude of wonder, curiosity, and interest, then the process begins when questioning begins. But questioning already presupposes some presentation, some data of consciousness towards which one's attention has turned and about which one is asking the question. Query may stop with indifference, boredom, or distraction, but these do not resolve it. Query is resolved by an insight, a possible answer to a question of the form, 'What is this?' An insight presents a coherent content that is not some further act of perception, but an act of conception or understanding. But then the spirit of inquiry only changes its level of concern and, reflecting upon the content of the insight, continues to wonder, 'Is this really the case?' Here, query seeks reasons for assent and, formulating the insight into a conditional, seeks the fulfilling conditions that would provide those reasons. This will necessitate a return to presentation (*phantasm*) for at least part of those fulfilling conditions. Thus, the process cycles from attention to the data of presentation through insight induction to re-formulation, critical reflection, and perchance the grasp of an unconditioned propositional content. A bright idea has become knowledge. But the inception of a justified truth claim, whether written, spoken, or merely thought, will become the data of further questions for understanding and questions for judgment, and so the process of coming to know may form a self-correcting process of learning that heads towards the ideal limit of 'no further relevant questions,' a state only attained by exhaustive knowledge.

How the process can be said to 'cycle through itself' bears repeating.

Lonergan called it a *dynamic process* of coming to know. For the distinct levels of cognition should not be imagined as static faculties, with consciousness being shunted from one to the other. Rather, the notion of discrete levels is a useful schema that emerges through a phenomenological analysis of an ever-ongoing process of human intelligence on the move. The key to understanding what is meant by the process of 'cycling' through stages is the link between the fourth level of decision (and consequent action) and the first levels of attention to data, the way that the product of the fourth level becomes the data of a new iteration (or altered manifestation) of first level *phantasm.*

Here is how this works. The first level is the stage of intelligent attention and inquiry directed towards the data of presentation. Something is present to us in consciousness, towards which we may direct attention and concerning which we may have an insight. For example, suppose these data are the sounds crackling through an old walkie-talkie. On the second cognitive level, insight posits that the irregular crackling is not mere static, but a weak and distant voice, perhaps. But is this indeed the case? We formulate a condition for assent: if on the one hand, static can be reduced, the voice would be isolated; if on the other, the pulsing recedes along with the static, there was no voice. Moving the antenna around will often reduce static. Therefore, in order to come to the third level of reflective judgment, we must see whether or not the voice-like crackling will remain when the static is reduced. All that is now required is a fourth-level mental act: a decision, the choice to act and to begin repositioning the walkie-talkie to new angles, say. But now the selfsame action of moving around the antenna (thereby reducing static), while fulfilling the conditions for assent, is also an alteration of the data of presentation, for now the walkie-talkie and the listener are in different positions, and this observable change is on the level of things to which we may attend (level one). The new position is revealed by the new data in consciousness, in which we are aware of locomotion and orientation. By attending to these new data and comparing them with the memory of the previous position, we may conclude, 'We changed position, reduced static, but the supposed voice disappeared as well.' Therefore, the initial insight of 'Aha, this could be a voice!' has been sufficiently falsified. Thus, the process is said to cycle through itself, for in acting upon judgment (the fourth level of decision), whether by thought, word, or deed, one is changing the way *phantasm* appears, and this presents new data for attention. We return to level one, completing a cycle.

I have presented this system of dynamic cognitive action in a theoretical and formulaic manner. In reality, however, Lonergan's generalized empirical method is always the actual operations of some particular human subject, living in a historic and cultural context, within a web of intersubjective relations. Aside from the social nature of knowing implied in this, there is the role of emotion and desire as part and parcel of being a healthy human subject. Emotions too are valid parts of the human cognitive process.

Emotions delimit our sphere of concerns and reveal to us a universe of value. While emotions will depend upon judgments of fact to interpret the presentations of *phantasm*, intentional objects are greeted with de facto value apprehensions embodied in our emotional responses. While emotion and desire may present us with possible objects of choice and action, the judgment of value determines the distinction between merely apparent values (objects that merely satisfy) and genuine values (real human goods). The final determination of the good is achieved in a decision and action, for the good is always concrete and is not manifest until action chooses, not merely when emotion and judgment affirms. Thus, there is the possibility that we may apprehend and judge the good, yet fail to perform it. True moral development is achieved in a deliberation that leads to action, and not one that merely asserts the right choice without action.

Behind all of this is an impulse – the pure desire to know – a manifestation of dissatisfied intelligence on the move. We do not turn around and see the pure desire to know by introspection; we grasp it insightfully as the immanent operator that awakens us from indifference to attention and concern, that would pose questions and become restless until answers are proposed, and that in seeking to know, would also seek to know value and the genuine good. Thus, human intelligence is active and heuristic at its core. This is what sets in motion the dynamic of all our various discursive methods of knowing: a primordial orientation towards appearances that only rests when it attains the actual, the genuine, the true, and the good.

Criticism and Defense of the General Theory

At least two criticisms of Lonergan's theory arise immediately. The first regards the universal nature of the method. Is it not the case that the generalized empirical method is so general that it amounts to platitudinous assertion of motherhood rules such as, 'Be attentive, be insightful, reflect critically, deliberate responsibly'? These are so broad as to be empty of any real guidance for just how we should proceed. The second criticism regards the method itself. It is one thing to describe what we in fact do when we go about learning and building blocks of knowledge, but what validates this as a prescriptive norm, as the method of all methods?

The first criticism makes perfect sense if we were expected to take these prescriptions as they stand and directly build from them, say, macro-economic theory or Kepler's solar system. But while I have necessarily presented Lonergan's cognitive stages in theoretical form, he derived them by insight into successful arts and sciences. It is through wondering how it is that the mathematician, the physicist, the sociologist, and even the phenomenologist achieve what they do that we can uncover the generically distinct kinds of cognition at work. Each of the specific disciplines is a specification of ways of attending to data found relevant to the question; of gaining and deploying insights that provide definitions, categories, and theories that define any discipline of learning; of attaining the judgments and conclusions that make up the knowledge unique to each discipline. Thus, Kepler's insights required attention to the new data made available in Brahe's astronomical measurements, data that together with mathematics prompted the insight that solar-centric orbits are elliptical rather than circular. But mundane inquiries such as finding out where one has left the car keys also exhibit the same pattern. For any activity in which we are learning or activating our knowledge, there will be a cycle involving attention to data, acts of understanding, acts of judging, and acts of deliberating and deciding. Thus, while it can be schematized in generalized terms, human cognitive process is always apparent as some more specific heuristic.

What this general schematization achieves is twofold: norms of completeness and norms of order. We are able, first, to see the dependency that each cognitive stage has upon the prior one, and hence a functional norm emerges. We cannot act responsibly without the facts; we cannot have the facts without valid judgment; we cannot judge a content that is irrational or self-contradictory; we will not have a mental content without some sensible presentation; and none of these operations will obtain or continue without some query or concern that is driving things. Thus, Lonergan's description provides the complete *set* of stages of operations. Moreover, this schema showcases the proper *order* within the set of operations for the inception of knowledge. Getting cognitive stages mixed up or skipping stages constitutes failure. We say that someone has jumped to conclusions, has been daydreaming instead of watching, or has presented an insight that is incoherent. The generalized empirical method imparts the norms implicit in the specific heuristics by which it is instantiated.

The second criticism can now be answered in light of my response to the first. Why should I accept the generalized empirical method as foundational to thinking, why not another method? Lonergan's response is that any theory that claims to explain human understanding and learning must account for its own inception and development and justification. Surely one cannot intelligently promote a knowledge claim about cognitive process that is not itself a product of that same process. Therefore, the real test comes from whether the system validates itself, or can be falsified by the sound operation of a counter-method. We discover the evident nature of cognitive method by attending to the data of our own conscious activity, by having insights into how insight happens, by wondering whether all this is indeed so, and by judging that indeed it is. The opponent, in order to deny that these are the normative stages of human cognition, will have to attend to the data of presented argument, to understand by means of insight just what the theory is, to then reflect upon whether it is true, and to find reasons for rejection. But these very acts of refutation are themselves an instance of the method, and hence refutation is impossible and revision will have to work with the same tools.

In this way, Lonergan shows that we have no business thinking we can *invent* the primary way of coming to know. If we are questioners and knowers already, and this is basically self-evident, then we must consciously and responsibly appropriate what we already do naturally and spontaneously. This is to take a conscious process and turn it into a self-aware, self-critical method. Simple as Lonergan's multi-stage dynamic process sounds, all accomplished branches of human knowledge have been the result of some specification of these operations.

The generalized empirical method is therefore the most fundamental set of intelligent activities, its order is normative, the pure desire to know that propels it is innate and is spontaneously operative (except among the mentally deficient), and the method is self-validating, attempts to refute it being self-destructive.[46] What we need to explore now is how this inescapable method is brought to bear upon the real-world applications of *phronesis.*

3

Lonergan's 'Common Sense Insight' and Its Relation to *Phronesis*

How does a maximally generalized method of insight induction work in the daily rough and tumble of ethical choices and decisions? In the light of Aristotle's ethical perception as well as Lonergan's general theory, I wish now to focus more precisely upon Lonergan's description of a kind of insight deployed against the concrete and particular circumstances of human living. I think that Lonergan's 'common sense insight,' together with his identification of the cognitive role of emotions, can be shown to be what the *phronimos* is activating when gaining ethical insight. Providing a comparison of common sense and *phronesis* is my goal here and allows me, in due course, to work out the ramifications for a theory of objectivity in virtue ethics.

Lonergan claims that his theory is grounded upon Aristotle's doctrine that *phantasm* is the precondition of any mode of thought, be it theoretic or practical.[1] For both Lonergan and Aristotle there is no such thing as imageless thought, and this means that some mode of presentation is always attendant upon the discovery of ideas, their recall, and their transmission. Furthermore, for both philosophers, part of the way presentation appears is predetermined by the cares and habits of the inquiring subject.[2]

The question then is, what are the concerns and questions that one should bring to the world in order that appearances be construed in such a way as to allow *phronesis* to operate? The rest of this chapter will attempt to show that according to Lonergan, the concerns ought to be the very ones immanent in what he called 'common sense insight,' but guided by an informed and unhindered thrust to realize the human good.[3] In the course of this presentation, the parallels to *phronesis* should become quite clear.

This chapter presents three major aspects of Lonergan's conception of practical intelligence and its apprehension of ethical salience: first, a description of common sense insight, that is, intelligence directed at concrete living; second, the phenomenal construing of the world: *phantasm* and Lonergan's theory of 'patterned experience'; and third, a careful look at the cognitive nature of emotion.

Common Sense: Intelligence Directed at Concrete Living

In the previous chapter, I presented the case of Helen Keller. Her experience of water and the inscribed 'W' was that which appeared to her in consciousness; that is, the *phantasm* towards which she directed her inquiring intelligence. Hitting upon her insight, Keller re-construed 'appearances' from perplexing sensations to meaningful presentations. She gained a new understanding of what was going on – namely, that someone was attempting to communicate with her, to teach her how to use signs. Three further examples of modes of insight occurrence may help elucidate Lonergan's conception of common sense intelligence in action.

The first example is military tactics. Due to the uniqueness of each actual battle, excellence in tactics only comes with past experience and acute assessment of the current situation. The expert 'sees' rather than deduces what is called for; victory goes to the one who sees soonest and applies his insights most swiftly. In tactics, all planning is contingent, and the tactician may be forced by events to improvise in unknown terrain.

The second example is medical diagnosis. Again, discovering what disease is ailing a patient requires at some point a direct insight into appearances. Drawing on her set of past experiences with similar symptoms, the various syndromes and classifications learned at medical school, and perhaps the extra eyes of her colleagues, the doctor is able to hit upon a correct diagnosis only by inspection of the case at hand.

A third type of example is more interesting. A businessman, perplexed by the peculiar loss of profits showing in the balance sheets and intrigued by the purchase, on company accounts, of one-way airline tickets to Mexico, suddenly reads the sly smile of his business partner for what it indicates: the partner is embezzling company funds and is about to escape its jurisdiction. It was the subtle nuance of the smile that illuminated and linked the other clues, and – aha!– insight is triggered. This is the intelligence deployed by the detective that enables him to 'see' X *as* evidence.

These examples all share at least the following elements. They involve attention to the configuration of particular things, relations, and events. They involve a query that seeks clues that would illuminate a whole network of relevant relations, thereby solving a puzzle. They are all types of knowledge that rely, for their excellent actualization, upon a bank of past experience with similar concrete particulars. They cannot be contained within the rules of a deductive science but deal with probabilities of insight induction that increase in direct proportion to the skill level of the practitioner. These examples would all be classed under Lonergan's general category for intelligence directed at particulars: common sense insight. Clearly, these are also all elements that Aristotle showed are active in *phronesis.*

Because practically minded individuals do not arise in isolation but from within families and other social groupings, common sense insight occurs as a partly *collaborative* enterprise. Initially, the mastery of concrete exigencies is learned by observation, imitation, osmosis, and instruction. Insight crystallizes in individual habits and skills and within the group as customs, traditions, and institutions. This means that however original an individual's own insight may be, it will also represent to some degree an incremental development of a socially constituted block of knowledge. Prime examples of this social type of practical intelligence are the manners and customs that configure human interaction. These can become very sophisticated, as for example in the social protocol of shame cultures, or in the subtle but definite awareness of what is acceptable in style and fashion. Were an outsider to enter, her obvious lack of participation in the common sense of the group would soon set her apart.

Clearly, then, it makes no small difference into which set of common values, assumptions, habits and traditions one is born and reared. For the first skill set one will acquire is the skill of coexisting (and then perhaps excelling) within the group, and whatever personal modification of the skill set one might add would develop dialectically with the group. Otherwise, ostracism may result. In the end, the mature person of common sense does not break free with god-like independence from social living but becomes a paragon of virtue for his companions. Common sense intelligence, then, does not make one a rugged survivalist, but a politically and socially viable constituent of one's group.

The Method of Common Sense Insight

The demarcating factor in expertise is just that ability of allowing relevant past experience to come to the fore while confronting new situations, thereby imparting a kind of perception-like direct grasp of what is called for. Such a set of past insights, insofar as it fails instantly to yield a suitable answer to the query sought, Lonergan called an *incomplete* set.[4] It is incomplete simply because it does not contain the precise insight needed to master *this* case. If it did contain the needed insight, there would be no inquiry, no scrutiny of the case, no deliberation; rather, there would be competent immediate action. This is the case for any skill that is being actuated, such as driving a car. We do not deliberate or wonder what to do when we see a stop sign; we spontaneously act from an acquired habit. The needed insights are operative semi-consciously, perhaps, and our skill set is complete and adequate for the driving scenario we face. It is only when we come across the unexpected – an unfamiliar sign – that our skill set is said to be incomplete with respect to that particular situation.[5]

It is precisely by using the incomplete set to induce the needed insight that the expert finds solutions to ad hoc circumstances. The methodology of common sense is to exploit, through the encounter of this incomplete set with the new concrete configuration of salient features, the *probabilistic* nature of insight occurrence. For the greater one's experience base, the higher the probability of suitable insight induction. Understanding *why* insight occurs through the presence of an incomplete set of past similar experiences is unimportant to the functioning of common sense; that insight can and often does according to some degree of probability is what is being deliberately harnessed by the person of common sense.

When a practical insight does occur, that insight alone is not some permanently accessible 'right answer.' The insight is recognized to be correct because it both coheres with the prior partial set and it connects that whole set to the situation at hand. Expertise cannot be contained in a single insight, only in a *set* of past insights. It is this newly completed set of relevant insights that 'fits' the situation, and now what needs doing seems obvious. The set of previous similar insights are now freshly co-coordinated and rendered directly pertinent through the adjustment provided by the newest situationally induced insight.

Once such a key 'set-unifying' insight has been discovered, reconsidered, tested, and affirmed – whether through deliberation, imagination, comparison, consultation, or any other method of verification or corroboration – it becomes part of the set of all insights and part of the latent experience of the agent; the newly modified insight set now reverts to a state of incompleteness vis à vis the next concrete exigency. Clearly, the broader one's base of experience and the greater one's access to the experience of others, the higher will be the probability of success in common sense insight induction.

Finally, with any practical insight concerning action one can ask a question quite distinct from the question of success and utility. One can ask, 'Should I, in fact, do X?' and, 'Would doing X really be worthwhile?'[6] Without this value-laden question for deliberation, common sense insight would seem more like shrewdness (*deinotes*) than *phronesis.* To differentiate the moral use of common sense insight from an inductive art such as diagnosis, there needs to be this questioning that *seeks* genuine value, along with a reliable ability to *discern* genuine value. It is here, if not before, that the subject must rely upon inner states and dispositions, such as feelings of preference, memories of shame and praise, responsibilities and obligations to family and friends, tribe, corporation, and so on. One hears the voices of conflicting desires and is forced to adjudicate them within an unsettled conscience.[7] Lonergan argued that some emotions play a vital role in the *apprehension* and *judgment* of value. For our emotions are often the first clue that what we value is relevant here, even before we can articulate it, and they send us into reflection and deliberation precisely to uncover that value. This process receives more discussion later on.

In summary, the practical insights of common sense are insights gained under the exigencies of concrete living, where actions are construed by our past experiences, our desired futures, and our current social relations. Because of the contingent nature of human affairs, no set of past common sense insights is complete, for each new state of affairs requires just those additional insights that would link past experience with current demands.

Common sense insight has these defining features:

> (1) It is an intellectual habit, an excellence in induction that produces practical truths.
> (2) It concerns itself with concrete living, not productive art and not theoretical understanding.
> (3) It relies upon the insight-inducing capacity of an ever-growing block of past experience with similar particular scenarios.
> (4) It is concerned with personal action, choice, and decision. It is not primarily concerned with what others should do or what is universally called for in human action but asks, 'What should *I* do? How does this affect *me*?'
> (5) While it can generate real knowledge, common sense can do so *without* producing general theories, universal definitions, or absolute imperatives. Common sense is not concerned with schemas of explanation and prediction. Rather, it sets out to master concrete particulars and hence develops systems of insights only derivatively.
> (6) When it does work with sets of insights, it produces only rules of thumb, proverbs, and parables, all non-binding but worth keeping in mind.[8]

Construing the World: Lonergan's 'Patterns of Experience'

The way things appear is determined, to some degree, by the character of the observing agent. And character is a habituated tendency of the emotions and the desires towards certain preferences and choices. As Aristotle put it, to the lover of horses, horses appear desirable and good.[9] Lonergan has his own version of this doctrine. Not only does the order of discovery entail that *phantasm* is a prior necessity for insight, but for him, too, the most basic drives, desires, and concerns of the subject condition the way the world appears. Axiomatic for Lonergan is the idea that intelligence becomes focused and deployed methodically when there is a fundamental *desire* at play: a pure desire to know, to understand, to be rid of uncertainly and perplexity. This general desire is made determinate through more specific modes of epistemic desire; that is, desire to know the truth, desire to master a skill, desire to behold beauty – but also, desire to live well in general.[10] And for every mode in which inquiring desire might be manifest, there is a corresponding way in which that inquiry itself construes the world, construes the set of data we consciously experience.

Lonergan calls these most general kinds of construal 'patterns of experience.'[11] Such construals of the world, whatever the contribution of the subconscious, will be had within conscious experience. From the subjective side, there is a distinct aspect to modes of consciousness that allows us meaningfully to categorize one moment as practical experience, for example, another as intellectual experience, another as mystical experience, and so on.[12]

From this phenomenological fact, Lonergan makes at least four basic claims regarding such patterning. First, consciousness is experienced, at various times, as having several general kinds of patterning. Second, what identifies a pattern is its linked network of general kinds of salience. Third, kinds of salience are the intentional correlates of the most general kinds of desire, concern, interest, or goals of the subject. Fourth, human consciousness is experienced as constantly shifting between one or more dominant patterns of experience (Lonergan's 'polymorphism' of consciousness).

Consider a 'flow of consciousness' such as that described by William James, a flux of mental data within which we limit our focus by acts of attention.[13] Lonergan accounted for the attention/inattention of salience selection by linking that process to the subject's most fundamental concerns, and these will predetermine to a large degree the general patterns of our conscious experience. In providing some examples of what Lonergan has in mind, I offer only the following four basic concerns of the subject and their correlative patterns of experience.[14] First, desire to comprehend and know the real from among the apparent or confusing yields the *intellectual* pattern of experience. Second, desire for the pleasant, the enjoyable, for play and spontaneity yields the *aesthetic* pattern of experience. Third, desire for the satisfaction of animal urgencies yields the *biological* pattern of experience. Fourth, concern for success and development within intersubjective, pragmatic, and concrete affairs of life yields the *dramatic* pattern of experience. As will shortly become plain, common sense insight is most likely to occur in this fourth pattern of experience.

The Intellectual Pattern of Experience. Consider this illustration: Desiring to learn some philosophic truth, one enters a library to study an ancient manuscript, say Eriugena's doctrine of divine foreknowledge. After beginning to concentrate, one is drawn into the terms and concepts of the exposition and is lifted into the abstract ether of speculative philosophy. What becomes salient here are sound premises, valid inferences, careful distinctions, grammatical nuances, and theological presuppositions. Other concerns have receded to the periphery of awareness – that is, one no longer senses one's hunger or the sounds from outside the room. One's awareness is restricted and delimited to what Lonergan calls the intellectual pattern of experience; the intentional objects that dominate this pattern are symbols, abstractions, critical procedures, and the like. Such objects of intellectual concern, linked together and illuminated as salient, form a distinct pattern of experience.

The Aesthetic Pattern of Experience. Now, suppose one becomes distracted by the fine uncials in the script, the illuminated characters, the smell of the old parchment, and the gilt page edges. One is amused by the intricacy of the work; admiration for the artistic skill emerges, as does, perhaps, a sense of privilege at being near such an ancient creation. One has now shifted, according to Lonergan, into the aesthetic pattern of experience. The relevant and linked items of this pattern include the concrete data of proper and common sensibles, form and accuracy of workmanship, and the emotions associated with admiration and pleasure. Insight interprets our emotions as approval; there may be a desire to posses the fine object. The general field of salience is the pleasant, the surprising, and this is so even when what we find beautiful is something theoretical or abstract in itself.

Keep in mind that within both intellectual and aesthetic patterns of experience, as with the rest, essentially the same empirical data dominate the sensible field. Yet the a priori concerns of the subject, by illuminating and prioritizing different features of the phenomenal field, superimpose a network of salience that construes the same sensible data as a distinct pattern of experience.

The Biological Pattern of Experience. Suddenly, without warning, the librarian just attacks you! The fight or flight response kicks in. Sensible acuity is heightened; fear charges the body with adrenaline and you sense agility and energy. Insight identifies threats to avoid and possible routes of escape – and all with little or no intellectual calculation. You have entered a primal biological pattern of experience. This pattern, being concerned with no ulterior purpose but immediate biological need, radically alters the topography of salience. Within this pattern, Eriugena's heavy tome suddenly and obviously takes on an identity as a weapon or shield; theology and artistry have been deselected from attention. Insight identifies previously unthinkable options, such as mightily tossing the book at your assailant. This radically different salience network is determined by the dominant concern of survival. Actions are instinctive and reflexive rather than conscious and deliberate.

The Dramatic Pattern of Experience. You escape and make it out onto the street, gradually calming down as you feel safety return. Knowing, of course, how public transit works, you successfully manage to take the bus home, reflecting upon what to do next. You know how to use a phone so you call a friend. You discuss the case in the light of your society's notions of crime, madness, and the minds of librarians. You think about what a good citizen should do, what kind of person you would be if you failed to report the incident. You take the time to figure out that new coffeemaker, and then you brew a cup and think things over. You remember that you were once a librarian too, and that rare manuscripts should not be handled without special permission. The situation shifts: it dawns on you that perhaps an apology on your part is more appropriate than filing a complaint. But perhaps sleeping on it is best; you'll decide in the morning. For you have returned to the dramatic pattern of experience from where we work out the particular concerns of daily living and personal development.

Although dramatic living is neither simply an intellectual, aesthetic, technical, nor a biological activity, notice how it may utilize all these capacities in harmony, towards some ulterior end. For in the dramatic pattern above, you utilized past experience (using a bus and a phone), technical or intellectual knowledge (getting that coffeemaker to work), intersubjective social attachment (relying upon friends for their emotional and experiential support), and biological needs (requiring sleep to facilitate sound judgment). The concerns of dramatic living coordinate these functions towards its own proper end: living successfully, living well.[15]

All four of these examples exemplify Lonergan's notion of a pattern to describe a network of linked salient features that characterize our most general modes of conscious experience. The type of pattern of experience one finds oneself in will determine, according to some statistical probability, the kinds of insight one is most likely to attain. Thus within an intellectual pattern of experience, one is much more likely to grasp intellectual insights, though it is always possible that a particular formula might trigger a reminder to pick up milk on the way home. Or again, one may be daydreaming in the aesthetic pattern of experience, and yet see in the embers of the fireplace a *phantasm* that triggers the insight into the structure of a chemical compound, as in the case of Friedrich von Kekule cited in chapter 2.[16] Within the dramatic pattern of experience, one deploys knowledge and experience in order successfully to decide, act, and live. This agenda will select its own corresponding web of salience.[17]

The dramatic pattern of experience also seems to be a kind of 'default centre,' an equilibrium we return to simply because we are biological and social creatures who must live out our lives in particular and intersubjective situations. Failing to return to the common sense of the dramatic pattern is ultimately detrimental to the goal of successful living, for we cannot survive long in the narrow confines of strictly intellectual patterns, nor in the dreams of the aesthetic pattern, nor the in brute wildness dictated by biological urges. The dramatic pattern is the place from which we may best decide the times and manners in which, say, biological and intellectual pursuits can play their good and appropriate roles – as part of life as a whole.[18] For the dramatic pattern is invoked by the basic concern of moment-by-moment living as well as by today's concerns for future living, and thus it will be a centre from which other, more specific (or less rational) concerns must be balanced, managed. This is what *phronesis* does, and so the dramatic pattern of experience seems to be the appropriate pattern of construed intentionality from which it would operate.

Patterned Experience versus Narrative

With the notion of patterns of experience in mind, we can better see the place of narratives. First, however, we can consider how Aristotle's geometric insight analogy may be deceptive: the objects of ethical perception are just not as simple as geometric shapes. Perhaps a momentary state description of a scenario might be analogous to a geometric shape, or to the static relations between figures in a photograph. But as noted earlier, Nussbaum and Sherman suggest that ethical salience comes from insight into scenarios that are much more like stories than photographs. Getting it right in the empirical and descriptive field of ethical investigation involves following the narrative's unfolding plot in its proper direction, order, and interrelations. The narrative process itself specifies and elaborates general ends to which we are committed and builds a mutual support among them. Out of this process, salience can emerge in a way that is impossible for simple state descriptions.[19] Thus, Sherman approves of Dancy's notion that the justification of one's ethical decision is not achieved by appeal to a universal principle but is a matter of persuading someone to see things in the right way.[20]

What counts as right will be determined by a well-developed competency for discerning moral properties and using moral concepts.[21]

Nevertheless, my critique here is that while we may discuss narratives from the 'outside,' so to speak, making objects of the actors, events, settings, actions, and the like, we do not actually *live* through a narrative per se; we live through a sequence of patterns of experience. This is something overlooked in Nussbaum's and Sherman's discussions. It is only when we reflect upon and/or recount our experience to others that we produce something like a narrative. Producing a narrative is a second order creative and interpretive act, distinct from the direct insightful understanding of our experience as we encounter and master it.

Nussbaum's 'interpretive seeing,' then, cannot refer to a narrative, but is the prior correlation of insightful perception into desideratively construed appearances. True, the intelligibility of what we immediately grasp in that way may be incommunicable without narratives, but these then are tools for reflective understanding or for communication to others. It seems, then, that mastery of the concrete requires a dialectical reference between dramatic living and narrative reflection – a process already said to be intrinsic to ongoing *phronesis.*

The distinction between reflective narratives and directly lived experience raises some interesting problems also overlooked by Nussbaum and Sherman. For while a narrative may adequately capture the sequence and salience of some lived event, its use will be affected by the dominant pattern of experience we are in when reflecting upon it. A common negative case is the tendency for over-intellectualized responses to narratives that should demand, from a virtuous person, an emotive interaction. Without intending to be heartless, one could be listening to descriptions of terrorist violence and instantly shunt the details into historical and political categories of analysis, thus failing to register outrage or other pertinent emotional judgments. Or again, in the recreational concerns of the aesthetic pattern of experience, one might take up a narrative for the sake of entertainment and fail to register the exploitation or vulgarity involved, because one is caught up in the artistic merit of the work. While the intellectual and aesthetic categories are valid in themselves, presumably, ethical wisdom should at least jolt us into knowing when our pattern of experience is hindering instead of helping us register ethical salience. To know, therefore, that we live our lives in constantly shifting patterns of experience brings with it a responsibility to be aware of the advantages and the blinders associated with each of these frames of mind.[22] If there is a responsibility to narrate accurately or well, there is an equal responsibility to listen appropriately during collaborative deliberation. *Phronesis,* it would seem, demands self-knowledge here. For the pattern of experience that dominates our 'interpretive seeing' at any given time influences the way we would 'read' a reflective narrative, and this means that narratives and patterns of experience complicate any account of being 'morally objective.'

Emotions and the Problem of Bias

The role of emotions in judging value, and hence in playing an integral part in any theory of objectivity in a virtue ethics, will be dealt with more fully in the next chapter. What I want to present here are two of Lonergan's points for comparison to Aristotle's view that our desires and aversions will tend to make their objects seem pleasant or unpleasant to us, and this will affect how wisely we may judge their real value. First, emotions do have some share in the rational faculty; that is, they perform some cognitive function and convey content. Second, emotions play a central role in the vicious malformation of cognition, the flight from insight that leads to bias, injustice, and personal and institutional blindness and decline.

With respect to the first point, it is significant that Lonergan was one of the first in the field to include emotional intelligence in human cognition of value. Beginning in 1959 but coalescing by 1972 in *Method in Theology*, his theory identifies human feelings as central to the apprehension of value and the judgment of value.[23] A feeling is always an apprehension of something that is valuable to *us*, important to *us*, salient to *us*. It is a response to intentional presentation, and whatever faculties may be involved in apprehending the intelligibility of intentional objects, it is emotion that will usually register the value of the presentation to the conscious subject. Somatic feelings, such as hunger or discomfort, and general moods, such as depression or irritability, are excluded by this definition.

But apprehension is not the same as affirmation.[24] We apprehend that X is valuable to ourselves through the initial emotive impact its appearance has upon us. But upon reflection, we discover that what is really good for us is actually something to which we have a strong aversion, say, dental surgery. Still, in order to decide that indeed we shall visit the dentist we will be relying upon emotion again, directed towards the imaginary presentation (*phantasm*) of some future state in which our teeth do not hurt. Emotion will play a role in apprehension of value, but also in the reflective judgment of value as well. For while emotion may initially apprehend value, Lonergan did not think that it is up to intellect alone to judge value, for value judgments differ in important ways from fact judgments.

The second point to make is that since emotion can register value, a disvaluing or a repression of emotion may lead to serious cognitive impairment. This idea is covered in Lonergan's extensive treatment of bias.[25] For bias has a tendency to arise most easily within common sense thinking, under the limitation of utility criteria and the limited experience base of any single human group.

Dramatic bias is perhaps the unavoidable consequence of our intersubjective social development. For just as every group embodies a set of common sense insights that have survived the attrition of time and pragmatism, so too each group's set of acquired and tested practical insight inversely reflects a body of rejected concerns, unasked questions, scorned sentiments, and ignored presentations that are transmitted between members and generations. Thus, each individual never does start life with a clean slate but with a block of pre-critical assumptions of what is worth asking or worth feeling.

Individual bias, which can be considered a form of egoism, is defined by Lonergan as an incomplete development of intelligence, for one may really discover what is good for oneself, but stop short of considering whether this is compatible with social living.[26] Egoism is in part the result of an incomplete consideration of the full human good, whereby the very real goods that impinge upon the self are given a dominating place in the overall schema of goods that include other individuals as well.

But deeper even than such partial repression of questions and salience, a tendency that comes from inordinate consideration of self, there may arise the total repression that comes from active 'flight from insight itself.'[27] Just as the generalized empirical method when operative embodies a drive towards being, towards the real, so too the many ways that people become neurotic and bigoted embody an active principle of *aversion* to certain insights. Whether through fear, hatred, revulsion, pride, or some other pathology, there is the phenomenon called *scotosis* – a darkening – whereby the images, presentations, or scenarios that would likely trigger certain insights are repressed, denied, censored, or disguised.[28] This can happen in neurotic repression, where the dreaded object will simply not be phenomenally available to consciousness, leading to untold cases of personal suffering and destruction.

But such a need to repress insight-triggering *phantasm* can become a social and institutional malady as well. We see this in the sly use of euphemisms that only connote the desired slant on things, and more seriously, in the silencing of symbol and expression by totalitarian and fundamentalist fanaticisms. There may be cases where, in direct conflict with a pure desire to know, there is operative a deep desire *not* to know, a desire to flee from unwanted or threatening insights. Such bias against well-ordered cognition can exist within the individual, the group, and the entire culture.

Group bias is distinct from the neurotic bias above. It is the dramatic bias as it functions within a group rather than in an individual. Group bias means, 'This is the way *we* do it around *here*, mate.' While often highly efficient 'the way *we* do things' is not by itself a valid yardstick for judging new circumstances and actors. The dialectic of community is such that 'our way' comes into conflict with 'their way,' and either we have the survival of the fittest or we need to seek a more comprehensive viewpoint that might integrate the various communities of common sense that develop among larger societies.

Whereas individual and neurotic bias may lead to attitudes that conflict with ordinary common sense, group bias operates in the very genesis and preservation of common sense viewpoints.[29] It is precisely the intersubjective emergence of the 'way we do things' that gives it such resilience to external influence. For to each group, their own way just seems obvious, and a potent sense of apparent validity comes with mutual support from peers.

Problems arise when several different social groups emerge, each with a common sense that is not integrated by any higher viewpoint. Collectively, all these groups contain a myriad of practical insight, but precisely because they are subdivided into groups, distinctions of class, function, and power emerge spontaneously. For by their sheer size, talent, opportunity, and other advantages, some groups will be better positioned to impose their common sense solutions upon the whole, or at least to have an inordinate, if unintended, dominance. However insightful these viewpoints might be, they have not been made socio-politically dominant by some overall theoretical, moral, or utilitarian agreement, but by the fact of power and social opportunism. It is not the best ideas that win out, but the ones that survive inter-group pressures and come out on top. This is the logical result if nothing else is operative in a society apart from common sense and personal interest.[30]

But this very process invites its own reversal through dialectic action.[31] For by force of argument, increase in numbers, and/or threats of various kinds, disgruntled groups may eventually become social facts that demand practical attention from the other groups, or the ruling group. Common sense pragmatism realizes that the disturbing groups need to be dealt with, at least for reasons of social peace if not for the merit of their ideas.

The response of groups to each other may take any form along the spectrum from progressive to reactionary. Ideas may be repressed by the dominant group, or absorbed, adapted, or sublated towards that higher viewpoint that would seek some mode of accommodating the perennial emergence of new insights.

The practical solution to this social exigency will be some form of systematizing both enfranchisement and principles of change, such that the natural propensity for sub-grouping and diversification will not be suppressed but channeled to the benefit of all. This may be a political ideal, but it is also a practical one, and therefore, presumably, were we ever to attain it, it would seem like the 'common sense' thing to do.[32]

General bias is the prejudice of pragmatic intelligence against theoretical and speculative modes of intelligence in general. This is what killed Socrates; it is the practical 'realists' of the world triumphing over the dangerous dreamers and idealists. For from the exigencies of pragmatic mastery of the concrete, what earthly good is all that speculation? But the bias that declares we must be practical at all times fails to see the ultimate practical value of theoretical knowledge. For it is through theoretic knowledge that we may gain breakthroughs in understanding more clearly our human nature, the very basis of a virtue ethics.[33]

In all of this, it is clear that emotions play a central role in the maintenance of each level of bias. There is an angry impatience with those who 'just don't see it our way.' There is fear of change, of the shame of being mistaken, of the short-term resistance to needed institutional change. There is the pleasure of power and the comfort of the received privilege. As many emotions as can be evoked to incite change, say by Aristotelian rhetoric, can also be used to maintain the status quo.

Yet there is also the emotional exuberance of exploration, the joy of discovery, the confidence of mastering large blocks of knowledge, and these too are feelings that foster honest inquiry and welcome new insights. The love of the truth is a corrective force, if not a decisive one, in counterbalancing the tendencies of negative emotion. Thus, I must end this discussion on bias with a positive word for emotion, lest we become biased against its legitimate place in ethics.

Emotions are a vital part of apprehending and judging the world of value. And our emotions are as much a reflective indicator of our own character development for Lonergan as they are for Aristotle. Questions of attaining moral objectivity in any ethic that relies upon subjectively conditioned emotional construals and perceptions will have to deal with the problem of bias. Sherman notes that 'in Aristotle's account, the *phronimos* or person of practical wisdom will need to correct for biases and preferences that interfere with the deliberation at hand; but recognition of this never leads to the identification of the impartial point of view with the point of view of ethical assessment in general.'[34]

The impartial point of view is a model of objectivity that excludes the emotions as well as the inclination and context of the agent; it is the objectivity belonging properly to, say, the science of physics. The *phronimos,* however, works against bias, not in an effort to attain the impartial view, but precisely by seeking to line up his partiality with what would be a genuine good in itself, and choice-worthy for that reason.

In virtue ethics, then, the conception of moral objectivity must include the notion of an ongoing, healthy functioning of subjective operations. One need not seek a god's-eye view of things; one need only have sufficiently corrected for bias to get the pertinent insight *this* time around. Habituation will increasingly lead the practitioner towards moral 'expertise.' Absolute objectivity is a chimera in this model; moral objectivity must become an ideal limit towards which individuals and societies head.

A Kuhnian Objection Considered

An objection to this model of moral objectivity may arise from the very basis of Lonergan's particularist method. For precisely by careful deference to attention, insight, and judgment, diverse blocks of common sense knowledge emerge but do not necessarily converge. Each could claim to be objectively or at least methodically arrived at, but may display irreconcilable conflicts with the other. If *phronesis* is a species of common sense, why would we expect the kind of convergence required for ethical objectivity? Perhaps the divergence of ethical theory and practice are the debris from some primordial unity (e.g., medieval Christendom). The history of ethics, then, may turn out to be a process of evolutionary replacement of one competing system with another, but with no obvious progress towards anything like moral truth.

Thomas Kuhn presents the structure of this kind of process. While there is a generally established canon of what we would call objective scientific criteria for theory selection,[35] Kuhn argues that the critical insight required for selection among competing alternatives may just as often be grounded in subjective factors of the agent. For instance, personal experiences and commitments such as political and ideological beliefs may impinge upon theory choice.[36] His notion of subjectivity, inherent in the logic of discovery, leads him to treat the choice criteria in theory selection as 'values' and not as hard rules; they cannot, therefore, be applied as an algorithm that determines the right or best choice.[37] Ethics may show the same pattern, for science and ethics are both human enterprises and the same human foibles may attend each.

A Kuhnian objection threatens the optimism with which common sense insight might aspire to moral truth or objectivity. Thus to deflect the threat, one must present reasons for believing in the likelihood of convergence towards a correct or unitary ethics, and/or show why a Kuhnian objection is off the point and applies to science only and not to ethics. Let me attempt both defenses.

Convergence. The ontological ground of the possibility of convergence in virtue ethics is the unity of human nature. Human nature is, however, developmental – both personally and historically. In the life of each person, humanity unfolds over time biologically and psychically, and this is why the final determination of whether *eudaimonia* has been attained must await the end of life. For only then will we have seen a fully lived instance of human nature. But humanity also discovers and actuates its potentials through historical, social, and cultural development. For example, the emergence of the division of labour and its specializations of thinking and acting reveal to us a far richer humanity than was obvious during, say, the Neanderthal era. One should expect, then, that human understanding of the good life would be something that unfolds in time as well. Nevertheless, this understanding still concerns the unity of human nature.

Furthermore, in *phronesis* we are talking about human action, not the selection of theory. The human action in question is the functioning of virtue as the primary means to *eudaimonia.* Since human nature is largely defined precisely by its unique function, and that function is singular or a single set of sub-functions, we can expect human flourishing to be the same general kind of thing for all humans.[38] To see how individual people have, in fact, developed and organized their capacities and circumstances into maximal flourishing will require attention to the particular case. We should expect surprises, but the logic will remain the same: virtue ethics is embodied in each person desiring rightly the things that are truly good for them and rightly averting from what is not. No more precision is possible.

If this is so, then the emergence of the various blocks of *phronesis* we might see both within and across diverse cultures and eras need not represent a threatening divergence into incompatible ethical phyla, but may rather represent the trial-and-error chunks of practical wisdom – some excelling where others fail – that we should expect from particularist methods. These need not converge eventually into a single world culture or 'way of doing things.' The convergence comes from something like an overarching society that can claim to be flourishing by means of the very differences that must remain because of concrete and particular variations among individuals and their circumstances.

Moreover, if the falsification of this notion of objectivity in virtue ethics is not to be found in the existing diversity of meta-theories,[39] would it perhaps be found in radically different understandings of the one human nature? For on the one hand, very significant differences in practical wisdom would emerge if underlying theories of human nature differ greatly. Even using the same *eudaimonistic* logic, cultures with, say, hugely diverse views of the place of women, children, and birth control, would no doubt develop divergent blocks of common sense insights regarding what is a good choice. These distinct societies and the *phronimoi* they produce might eventually become drastically incompatible, and the evolutionary model might mean the survival of the fittest, not the survival of the ethically most sound. Yet however dramatic such a clash may be, it will remain a clash of *interpretations* only, not a clash between *kinds* of human. Nevertheless, if errors of fact regarding our nature divide humankind, it will be through unbiased application of attention to data, insight, and reflective judgment, perhaps over many centuries, that we may arrive at a general acceptance of a unitary ethics most fitting for all humans.

On the other hand, radically diverse ethical views may actually reveal the presence of convergence on a deeper level even while divergence remains on the surface. For human ethical inquiry may head towards a unity of objectivity and truth because there is already a prior unity of values that is shared by all subjects who pursue the exigency to discover truth. Here is how this would work. Let us assume the principle that by willing part of an order one is implicitly willing the whole of the order. Then it follows that for two divergent ethical systems to compete and engage in genuine debate, there is an implicit affirmation of whatever prior conditions would enable such debate. Such prior conditions would include such obvious things as being alive in the first place and then becoming cognitively and intellectually competent. But these conditions presuppose and affirm the value of being nurtured and cared for while young and vulnerable, of being endowed with the accumulated set of presumed truths of one's culture and the commitment to uphold what is believed true and eschew what is false. This in turn implies a behaviour of loyalty to one's received values and a belief in the good of transmitting those values to others, which may have brought one to the debating table in the first place. Thus, even though divergence of moral insight may be apparent at the outset, there underlies any contest of views in pursuit of truth the shared values of being raised in ways congruent with inquiry and debate. One could not deny the moral goods of nurture, community, learning, loyalty, and intercommunication during this debate without contradicting one's own action of critical discourse. So then, convergence is not something that happens from ethical programs that begin as absolutely radically distinct, for the activity of human inquiry into the good shares foundational values with all communities that pursue it. This unity of conditions for the possibility of discovering the true and the good is also part of what it means to share in a unified human nature.[40]

Theory versus practice. We must distinguish between theory selection in metaethics and the deliberation and choices to be made by *phronesis.* We should not expect the canon for selecting explanatory frameworks to be the same as the method for detecting salience, desiring rightly, and choosing freely the elements of the good life. The former is a framework of axioms or putative laws under which data are comprehended, interpreted, and by which prediction is made and further fruitful understanding achieved. But the prior framework of virtue ethics is right desire, and this turns out to be a habit, a skill of detecting a mean between extremes. The good human life is not a theory to be selected, for we are not looking for an explanatory framework; rather, human flourishing is a way of *doing something well*; that is, living one's life well. Thus, scientific theory selection and ethical salience selection differ in kind: the goal of science is a form of understanding; the goal of ethics is a form of action.

Kuhnian anomalies are still a useful analogy, however, even in practical wisdom. Whatever ethical anomalies may bring about change or new insight in practical ethics, these will also differ in kind from theory anomalies, for they may not serve the same function of overthrowing entire paradigms as anomalies do in Kuhn's science. Practical ethical anomalies might look like a case of apparently genuine human flourishing utterly beyond anything 'our' culture could imagine.[41] It might even lead us to alter, say, our understanding of human nature (something science does occasionally), but this will not change the operative logic of virtue ethics, only the particular character of wise choices.

The Kuhnian type of objection, then, does not seem to apply to my approach to virtue ethics because it is not necessarily the case that divergence in ethics is the inevitable vector of history, and neither does the existence of divergent blocks of practical intelligence prove their ultimate incompatibility. For human nature is a shared unity. If it were not, we would merely develop a notion of the good corresponding to each kind of being – the good for man and the good for some other creature need not be generic, since we are not Platonists. Finally, metaethical theory selection and practical choices differ in kind. Kuhn is far more relevant to the former than the latter.

Summary

In the thought of Aristotle and of Bernard Lonergan, the following aspects of moral insight induction are basically the same:

(1) Emotion and desire participate in human rationality; they are cognitive of apparent goods, of things deemed important and valuable to us.
(2) Emotion and our states of preference and aversion affect to some degree the features of the phenomenal world such that a web of salience may be illuminated relative to each subject.
(3) This raises the question of distinguishing genuine good or value from merely apparent good or value, and this is a question of fact requiring the deployment of an intellectual habit. It also

> raises the question of calculating appropriate means to attaining genuine and concrete goods. Thus, insights pertaining to the good and what is conducive to it require a mode of intelligence calibrated appropriately towards mastering actual circumstances in the daily world of the subject.
> (4) The origin of such particularist insight, precisely because it is not deductive, relies upon past experience with similar scenarios to develop an 'eye to see.' The past grounds a sound pedagogy, which may lead to a terminal moment of direct insight into the concrete situation – an insight that is, perhaps, analogous to pattern recognition (including narrative forms).
> (5) The intellectual and desiderative virtues that accomplish this may develop into a habituated state of character not unlike expertise or connoisseurship. From this state, perceiving the good and choosing the good become increasingly automatic and pleasant.

Each of these points is generally descriptive of both *phronesis* and common sense insight. I think the primary difference is that common sense insight can include shrewdness as well, and hence *phronesis* is a species demarcated by the right desire for the genuine good, a concern absent from mere shrewdness. Still, I think it can be asserted that when the *phronimos* is 'getting it right' in ethical insight induction, she could be said to be successfully deploying the cognitive operation of Lonergan's common sense intelligence, though with an eye to what is good for her life as a whole.

But not enough has yet been said about the role of emotion and right desires in orienting the subject to the genuine good and to genuine value. Lonergan claims that emotions enable us to apprehend possible values and to judge real ones. But this is still too vague to assist us in linking emotion and objectivity in virtue ethics. Serious questions remain. Just what kinds of things are human emotions? Must they be consciously felt to count as emotions? Which emotions help us to become objective and which ones hinder? In what way are emotions said to be cognitive?

4

Emotive Perception of Value and Objectivity in Virtue Ethics

We have just seen that one type of cognitive malfunction is bias. Bias is tangled with emotion and often cuts short the open-mindedness of free inquiry. Clearly, if we can claim that there is a wrong way in which emotion affects judgment and perception, there must also be a right way. This chapter will turn to Martha Nussbaum's recent work on the cognitive nature of emotion and its role in discerning value, especially ethical value.

The goal of this chapter is to fill out more satisfactorily Lonergan's contention that in emotion we apprehend personal, yet actual, value. Nussbaum far surpasses Lonergan in working out concretely just how emotions and value are connected, and I will use elements of her work to augment Lonergan's theory. However, I will use Lonergan to re-insert a key distinction into Nussbaum's account, the distinction between *apprehension* of value and *judgment* of value. Finally, I will explore the contention of both Nussbaum and Lonergan that some mode of compassionate love may act as a genuine objectivity-fostering *phantasm*-construer. I will then be in a position to articulate what a fuller notion of 'being objective' would look like in the light of the foregoing.

Nussbaum on Emotions as Value Judgments

Martha Nussbaum's more recent ideas regarding the cognitive nature of emotions are of special importance,[1] and so I build on her work for several reasons. First, she has contributed largely to the Aristotelian framework of this inquiry and her discussion of emotions, drawing widely upon ancient sources, is quite compatible with a generally Aristotelian account.[2] Second, having been a major participant in discussions on the relation of emotion to *phantasm* and perception,[3] she has most recently contributed the thesis that emotions just *are* value judgments, and this represents a significant stance for understanding an emotion-dependent virtue ethics. Third, while Lonergan scholars have continually heralded his early recognition of the cognitive nature of emotion, and especially its cognition of value, Lonergan himself did so little to actually flesh out what he meant by this that his followers have been unable to agree upon just what he was getting at in his statement that 'between judgments of fact and judgment of value lies the apprehension of value by the emotions.'[4] Thus the third reason for concentrating on Nussbaum is an admission that any serious Lonergan scholar will now have to come to grips with the tremendous wealth of material that she has added to the philosophical exploration of emotion and value apprehension.[5]

Nussbaum's project opens with an argument against two contrasting views of the emotions: the non-cognitivist theory that emotion is a brute animal impulse which may respond somehow to what we think and perceive but which contains no rational or intentional content of its own; and the classical Stoic view that emotion is indeed cognitive – but always mistaken in each and every one of its judgments.[6] Against these views she develops what she calls the 'neo-Stoic' theory,[7] wherein the emotions are cognitive – they are in fact *value judgments* – but they are *not*, contrary to what the Stoics say, always wrong; in fact, they may be profoundly insightful in ways that only emotions can be.

If Nussbaum's project is successful, at least in a modified form, then it will go a long way towards developing a notion of objectivity in virtue ethics. Here is why. The model of cognition we have developed so far is based upon the general discursive principle of insight into *phantasm* (understanding) and critical reflection upon insight (judgment). That whole dynamic is dependent upon *phantasm*, and *phantasm*, as we have seen, is susceptible to alteration from at least three major forces: emotion, bias, and patterns of experience. If we can somehow compensate for or eliminate the distorting effect of these forces, we may achieve a functional dynamic that can meaningfully be called 'being objective.' Being objective will be understood negatively, as no longer being under the distorting influence of unsound emotion, bias, or the capricious influence of shifting patterns of experience.

Nussbaum argues that emotions are in fact judgments of value. She takes the same general position developed by Aristotle that emotions are intentional: they take objects; they can be 'about' things. Furthermore, she has argued in the past and now too that the intentional objects of thought are already pre-interpreted by emotion to some degree before we register them intellectually. The beliefs that can be embodied in emotion may be a very complex 'way of seeing' the object.[8] But Nussbaum now contends that emotions are more than just interpretations; they are judgments concerned with value, especially with things valued for their close connectedness to our own personal well-being.[9] She claims that emotions 'are forms of evaluative judgment that ascribe to certain things and persons outside a person's own control great importance for the person's own flourishing.'[10] And further, that 'emotions always involve thought of an object combined with thought of the object's salience or importance; in that sense, they always involve appraisal or evaluation.'[11] Finally, emotions are, in her view, actually *identical* with personal evaluative judgment.[12]

We can see that emotions are not the same as judgments that are, say, general ethical maxims such as 'Generosity is a virtue worth cultivating.' Rather, they are concrete judgments regarding things held dear to me on account of their relation to my own personal well-being. Emotions are an acknowledgment of my neediness and lack of self-sufficiency.[13] That is why the objects that are deemed important to my own *eudaimonia* and are vulnerable to loss (in ways that, say, good character is not) are objects about which I am prone to get emotional.

According to Nussbaum's interpretation of the Stoics, a judgment is an assent to or rejection of appearances.[14] This must involve two stages. First, there is an initial take on the world: this is the way that things appear to me. But so far, I have not yet accepted it. This is not necessarily a representational theory of perception; we are rather talking here about pre-critical presentation.

At the second stage, three possible roads open up. First, I can accept or embrace the way things seem; in this case the appearance has become my judgment. Second, I can repudiate appearances as false; in that case I judge them as contradictory. Third, I can let appearances hang without committing myself one way or the other; in this case I have no judgment or belief.

Aristotle gives an example of the second kind of judgment of appearances.[15] The solar disc appears to us as being roughly a foot across. Children might embrace this as the actual size of the sun. But if we hold the astronomically informed belief that the sun is, in fact, much larger, then we reject the appearance and embrace the contradictory. 'Assenting to or embracing a way of seeing something in the world, acknowledging it as true, seems to be a job that *requires* the discriminating powers of cognition. Yes, that's the way things really are ... [reasoning is] an ability in virtue of which we commit ourselves to a view of the way things really are.'[16]

According to this description, then, the assent of judgment is voluntary, an act of the will.[17] Yet it is not always deliberately performed: habit, attachment, or the sheer weight of events may extract assent from us. Children, who do not have the good sense yet to withhold assent, are still making a real judgment when they assent to the way things appear.[18] This model of judgment as assenting directly to appearances is then transposed to describe value-laden emotional judgments. An emotion such as anger, joy, or grief *just is* a personal embracing of the object of thought in a certain way.

How does this type of emotive judgment look in action? Nussbaum presents us with a tragic personal example of evaluative judgment: the death of her own mother.[19] Upon hearing news from her sister that their mother is gravely ill, Nussbaum becomes filled with the anxious possibility that Betty Craven, someone of enormous personal significance, is dead. This value-laden picture keeps haunting her, even though it is still the day before the actual death. As a report that evokes images and feelings, this is still considered by her to be at the stage of appearances, as in the solar disc example. Had she awoken from a nightmare or discovered the news to be a cruel hoax, she would have had reasons to reject the appearance. But as it happens, she eventually finds herself in a room with the body in front of her eyes and says, 'I embrace the appearance as the way things are.'[20] Her emotions record her sense of vulnerability and imperfect control. The emotion of grief itself is cognitive; it contains the intentional content that Betty Craven is dead. And it is cognition of that value-laden and lost person – *my* mother – that just *is* her grief.[21] Her grief is identical to the judgment that this was an externally valuable person to her. No additional cognitive step apart from the feeling needs to be added to attain that value judgment.[22]

Moreover, as this scenario shows, emotions as evaluations are always anchored in some human subject – they are *my* emotions, *my* value, *my* loss, says Nussbaum. Emotions contain an ineliminable 'me' to which projects, schemes, and whole life goals are intrinsically connected. This is not necessarily egoistic, it is eudaimonistic.[23]

Finally, emotional value judgments are still considered voluntary, at least in a weak sense. For while some feelings arise spontaneously and uninvited, it is still up to us to *acknowledge* them, to let them sink in and realign our lives. We may engage in denial of our grief, and hence fail to face up to the value we have just lost or to the vulnerability we fear. Thus even in the apparent spontaneity of emotion, Nussbaum finds room for the voluntary nature of judgment in our ability to accept or reject appearances.

This theory of judgment will be critiqued shortly, but for now I turn to the issue of truth and falsity in emotive judgment as Nussbaum presents it. Apart from the psychologically unhealthy acts of repression and denial, there are at least four further ways that emotive value judgments can err somehow.

First, there is the error of cognition, say, a *mistaken* belief that Betty Craven was dead, resulting in a grief that while not properly called 'false' would still be considered mistaken in terms of its propositional content: mother is dead. For the value judgment – mother is extremely important to me – is still correct. My having an emotion depends upon *what* I believe, not *whether* the belief is true or false.[24] Still, these are not errors of emotional feeling; what is felt would be perfectly appropriate were the content true. Emotions that go wrong because of factual error are really not mistaken, but misdirected.

Second, there is the error in evaluation itself: we must value things aright. There are things that are genuinely more important than others, say, mothers over hamsters. Something would clearly be wrong were we to grieve equally for a dead hamster as we would for our mother. 'Emotions have to do with what I, in fact, do value, however well or badly those things fit together.'[25] Error here presupposes some objective standard apart from emotion, but we will get to that later. Still, to grieve equally for a lost hamster is better called an inappropriate emotion rather than an untrue one.

Third, there is the error of failing to distinguish the effects of general versus specific feelings. This contrasting pair, as well as the next one, involves some subtle but important distinctions that are especially relevant to deliberation. We can have feelings regarding a person that are generally applicable to a large set of persons, in contrast to very specific feelings of the same kind directed uniquely at one person. If Nussbaum was grieved because a parent-as-mere-provider is missing, a role that any number of persons may fulfill, then this is not the same emotive judgment as grieving over 'this irreplaceable one person, my mother, who is now gone.'[26] Whether or not it is an error to evaluate a mother as a mere provider, this difference in emotive judgment clearly reveals an estimate of the mother's relative worth in one's view of flourishing; this evaluation reveals part of one's character and will impact deliberation. Therefore, whether an emotion is aimed at the general or the more specific must be taken into any account of emotional appropriateness.

Fourth, there is the error of failing to distinguish between background and situational feeling. This is not the same distinction as that just described. Background evaluations may persist through situations of numerous kinds, while situational evaluative judgments arise in some particular context alone. For example, suppose one has a fear of writing exams that is present in the background at all times, whether or not one is facing actual examination.[27] This may become manifest in certain behaviours: procrastination, general irritability, or snide remarks about the instructor, but the actual fear is background; that is, not consciously felt as such. Then, when faced with the actual situation of exam writing or when imaginatively thinking about it, one may experience an actual episode of such fear. Situational emotion is logically distinct from background emotion, yet both are ways of hating exams for both are in fact the same judgment manifest in differing modes. This is in contrast to general versus specific emotions, where the judgments involved are *not* the same.

This raises the question of whether there exists some single background emotion, or single set of background emotions, that would orient our whole perspective in a positive – even corrective – and ethically enlightening way. Lonergan clearly states that this is the case, that just as a basic emotion of fear or hate is the major factor in our biases, it is charitable love (Latin *caritas*; or Greek *agape*) that seems most likely to foster and maintain a healthy openness to truth and goodness.[28] Nussbaum, too, after several hundred pages that show the limitations of emotion and lead to the conclusion that 'no emotion is *per se* morally good,'[29] goes on to devote the second half of her book *Upheavals of Thought* to a detailed analysis of love as the main instance of background emotion and how it may indeed set us on the right track in ethical and political pursuits.[30] As this chapter proceeds, we will see how both of these thinkers conceptualize love as a background emotion and why it should perform the function of maximizing the probability of getting things right in ethical query.

But first, I must point out an error in Nussbaum. While all emotions are evaluative judgments, her full identity theory must be rejected, for it does not follow that all evaluative judgments must be emotions. The distinguishing factor for Nussbaumian emotive evaluations seems to be this: the things we become attached to because we deem them important to our personal well-being and yet deem them vulnerable to loss – these are the things we will emote about. For Nussbaum, emotion itself just *is* the embodiment of the personal-value-vulnerability aspect of the judgment. We *feel* it first, and then put it into propositional terms, say, as part of reflecting upon what it is we feel. However, value judgments that do not impinge closely upon the subject may not exhibit the 'feeling' factor of emotion or count as emotions at all, yet that does not make them any less judgments of value. For instance, preferences based upon aesthetic value may be personal yet need not involve emotion: my preference for symmetry in art is a value judgment that need not be connected to feelings of any kind, while the actual message content conveyed in the art may evoke strong emotion.

But Nussbaum does claim that emotive evaluation is a direct response to a phenomenal object or state of affairs 'seen as' having eudaimonic import. There is an appearance that strikes me as, say, tragic, and therefore I judge it to be bad for me. I may be mistaken, but I have passed a judgment intrinsically in my emotive response.

Augmenting Nussbaum: Apprehension of Value versus Judgment of Value

Here we face a complication caused, I believe, by Nussbaum's confusing of perception/apprehension and judgment *proper*. It is difficult to see much difference between Nussbaum's earlier concept of 'perceptual judgment' or 'interpretive seeing' and her recent theory of 'emotion as value judgment.' Both involve an immediate awareness of value in the very turning to *phantasm.* This value awareness is twofold. On the one hand, prior values and concerns to some degree already pre-construe the *phantasm* we encounter. On the other hand, emotive value judgments are responses to such an affected *phantasm,* making explicit, say, the things one holds dear and vulnerable. Emotion is at play in pre-construal as an apprehender and salience selector, and in any post-construal response.

Moreover, while in her earlier work *The Fragility of Goodness* Nussbaum did not make clear enough distinctions between perception and judgment,[31] in *Upheavals of Thought* she does not sufficiently clarify the distinction between emotively *recognizing* a *possible* value and the *judgment* of value itself.

Here, Lonergan's cognitive theory can help. As we saw, simply having a bright idea pop into one's head (insight of understanding) is not at all the same as having affirmed or denied that idea (via the insight that assent conditions have been met). So too with emotions: having a feeling may be a means of apprehending a *possible* value, but the judgment of value is a very different thing. Emotions may indeed register my sense of vulnerability connectedness, but this is just a general judgment about human neediness, not at all a reliable indicator of the value of the object presented.

Nussbaum would have done well to sharpen the difference between what we may call prima facie judgment and judgment proper. Prima facie judgment is not a true judgment, but is often a necessary heuristic stage in getting to a judgment. It plays a role similar to that of a supposition or a hypothesis – it supplies that content about which a judgment will be made. A prima facie judgment may very well be conveyed in emotion: I think of my dentist appointment and instantly shrink in revulsion. My emotion conveys the very plain content that I do not like the discomfort of dental invasion. The prima facie judgment here is, 'A dental visit is bad'; that is the evaluative content of the aversion. As an initial 'take' of the eudaimonistic state of affairs confronting me, this is at best a tentative judgment; that is, a proposition asserted precisely as pre-critical, as still requiring further reflection and verification. In fact, I am just restating the obverse of Aristotle's prima facie assessment of something as good when it is found pleasant and bad when found unpleasant.[32] These are initial takes of the world as it appears; critical reflection upon these feelings themselves may ultimately lead to the opposite judgment. Nussbaum seems to have lost sight of the distinction between pre-judgment and judgment *proper.*

Suppose my imagination or memory presents certain images of teeth with cavities, or perhaps I hear the distant sound of a small drill, when suddenly, bingo! – into my head pops the notion of a dentist appointment. This is a first order insight of understanding, a coherent content, and it now takes up the form of a presentation 'seen as' pertaining to me, and being an aversion of mine. I recognize in a vision of pain and discomfort a possible evil. Yet the critical turn that must yet be taken is a reflective judgment concerning the content of the initial take regarding dentist visits. Such a reflective query might be, 'Is it indeed the case that a visit to the dentist would be a bad thing?' This is just to restate the goal of value judgment, which is to discern the genuine value from the merely apparent one. In the initial take, what I recognize with a jolt of emotive force is that 'This impinges upon me!' The reflective judgment of a value is distinct from the initial judgment that something is in personal proximity to me.

In any emotive response involving pleasantness or pain, the outreach or recoil concomitant with the experience is *similar* to judgment; we are saying no to pain, yes to pleasantness in our responses. But this is perhaps only an analogy. It is *like* judgment but *not* judgment. What it shares with judgment is a kind of 'yes' or 'no' claim; how it differs is in how the yes or no is justified. In the case of emotion, either it simply is not yet justified at all, or some recounting of the history of the cognitive training of that emotion will have to be invoked as a supra-emotional justification for it. Emotional affirmation may be analogous to real judgment,[33] but it cannot be its own justification.

All this is to say that Nussbaum may be quite right that emotions are immediate judgments of personal and vulnerable eudaimonic values, but only if by 'judgment' is meant a kind of *tentative* assertion that still awaits a critically reflective act to become judgment *proper*. Emotion then is a kind of proto-judgment, coming before and being a necessary condition for personal concrete judgments of value, but emotion is not itself such a judgment. Rather, emotion is an immediate *apprehension* of a possible value, something that may turn out, in fact, to be a genuine good (or bad) for my flourishing.

Without this distinction, it is hard to know what Nussbaum means when she speaks of emotional evaluations being mistaken concerning things that objectively have certain values, but that we are valuing inappropriately (e.g., hamsters over mothers). For the criterion of evaluating one's own emotive evaluations cannot be further appeal to another emotion, for therein lies infinite regress. Neither can it be one of Nussbaum's 'background' values, for these may be just as inappropriate. Nor can it be some 'general' value, for in Nussbaum's theory I can value my Rolex watch generally as a good paperweight while failing to value it specifically as a gentleman's fine jewel attachment. That would be an error that is completely context relative, whereas mothers are always more valuable than hamsters. For the Rolex might one day be the perfect device for jumpstarting a failed engine during a life-and-death emergency, in which case its generic value as an electric conductor becomes situationally (yet also objectively) more valuable than its social status value. Thus, the judgment of value *proper* must be distinguished from whatever is being affirmed in emotional states of any kind.

Lonergan's judgment of value allows for this.[34] While Lonergan does distinguish between judgments of fact and judgments of value, this is not a radical fact-versus-value dichotomy, for there is still a real unity in the form and structure of the act of judgment itself. It is the insightful grasping of *reasons for assent,* not an act of the will to embrace appearance as Nussbaum describes it. And in judgments of value, the invulnerability criterion, as I see it, demands as a reason for assent the *absence of prohibiting conditions,* rather than the presence of sufficient conditions. Either way, judgment as a cognitive dynamic has the form of inference, not direct intuition.

This calls for a closer look. According to Lonergan's theory, the judgment of value is a variant of the three-stage cognitive method. Attention and query are directed towards appearances whose salience network is shaped in part by the character, experience, and beliefs of the subject. The question at hand might be, 'What should I do now?' and the answer may arise through common sense insight into the particulars being considered: 'Do X.' Critical reflection will ask, 'Should I *really* do X? Would it *really* be worthwhile?' At this point there is a major difference on the third level of critical reflection between fact and value judgments. For whereas in a judgment of fact, the insight is formulated into a conditional and the condition is met by a further turn to some concrete object or state of affairs whose being will be a reason for assent to fact, in the judgment of *value* there is no present state of affairs to which one may advert as a sufficient condition for assent. The reason for this is that fact judgments concern what is, and deliberation concerns what is not yet, but what is desired to be. Thus, the insight that would indicate a possible good choice or action must be affirmed in another way: by being invulnerable to reasons *not* to so choose or act. With this move, Lonergan keeps the structure of judgment-as-critical-reflection (not as direct assent to appearance) and yet makes sound judgments of value contingent upon the knowledge, experience, memory, habituation, and tastes of the person who would raise possible objections to action. For all of these expansions of a person's insight set will increase the probability of raising and answering sufficient objections. This is why, according to Aristotle, a more experienced person may be better at judgments of value, for he has an 'eye to see.' In a judgment of value, a hundred reasons *not* to proceed may be refuted, and yet there is always the possibility that we missed a fatal one. This too shows why we should not expect the same degree of clarity or accuracy in value judgments that we may expect from the sciences, empirical or otherwise.

Once we allow for the distinction between apprehension of value in a prima facie judgment and the judgments of value *proper*, then Nussbaum's discussion of emotion can be combined with Lonergan's notions of the problem of bias and the phenomenon of patterns of experience to lead us towards a critical view of 'being objective.'

Coming to Grips with Bias

Let me return to some aspects of the conception of bias we are using here. My interest is not to solve the problem of bias, but to point out what any solution would have to deal with.

I begin with a clarification. Bias is *not* a presupposition, so it cannot simply be a matter of holding the wrong one. Rather than consisting in an error of fact, bias is an emotional and reactionary response to social interrelations. There are four modes of bias explicitly dealt with in Lonergan's thought. First, there is the *dramatic bias* of personal living about which we have, initially, little control. There are then three often overlapping manifestations in which a personal bias can operate: as *individual bias*, placing myself against the world or against other parts of myself (egoistic and neurotic bias); as *group bias*, where it is my group against other groups, our ways against their ways; and finally, as *general bias* where one whole mode of being intelligent postures against other valid ways of deploying intelligence. An example is favouring common sense pragmatism over all other modes of thinking, be they intellectual, religious, artistic, or some other mode.[35] In any of its forms – whether individual, group, or general – bias can be manifest or masked in responses of arrogance, disgust, contempt, or hate. In whatever way it is manifest, bias is not a one-time expression but is a habitually conditioned state of emotive response. Thus, while biases may be reflectively understood and even critiqued, still they may remain stubbornly present as a harmful desiderative formation of the psyche.

The dramatic bias is a maladjustment of the dramatic pattern of experience,[36] that pattern of salience through which the concerns of concrete living are met, and it is common sense insight that masters the concrete. As we saw in the last chapter, common sense emerges as a non-systematic, flexible deployment of perception, past experience, and acquired coping techniques, all directed towards appearances with the goal of meeting practical exigencies. And it is precisely this nexus of pragmatically focused operative tools that gives common sense both its parochial genius and its propensity to exhibit dramatic bias. For prior to mastering the ad hoc concerns of one's family, village, tribe, nation, culture, and so forth, there is already at play *pre*-selection of values, a *pre*-selection of permissible questions, and the censoring of heretical doubts. Each culture rears the next generation with peculiar rewards and punishments aimed at manipulating emotive and behaviour responses, but these incentives and disincentives already embody a set of values and judgments. In other words, human understanding, by its very social emergence, will already be more or less closed to some insights that are not deemed relevant or acceptable to the group. This is not yet the deliberate manipulation of ideology, but the practical reality that we can only master a finite number of concerns, forcing us to prioritize the limited number of things we are able to cope with at any one time.[37] Thus prior to its later overt and conscious manifestation in the biases of egoism, group prejudice, and anti-intellectualism, dramatic bias is already at work covertly and unconsciously skewing the agenda of our practical intelligence. Clearly, this is much the same point we have been following in Nussbaum's notion of pre-construed *phantasm*, though from a decidedly negative angle.

Both Lonergan and Nussbaum place the distortion in large part upon the implicit judgments, and hence salience selection, of emotion and the truncated set of concerns surrounding personal survival. Nussbaum calls this a mild form of social constructivism.[38] She claims that all societies are the embodiment of implicit and explicit values and judgments of importance. The society into which one is born, therefore, insofar as it has any ability to shape the person, will to some degree shape the person's emotional beliefs and values. There can be socially pernicious emotions. There are good, bad, and in-between ways that societies promote or suppress certain emotions.[39] Therefore, the healthy development of emotions and their appropriate, or wise, expression in the ethical discernment of *phronesis* must overcome the dangers of bias. How can this be done?

We must realize what is *not* being called for here. Eliminating bias is not the elimination of 'our way of doing things' or 'our point of view.' It is the elimination of the fear or hate or suppressed wonder concerning *other* ways of doing things. Therefore, losing bias need not entail losing the pragmatic common sense that constructs 'our ways of doing things,' lest in removing bias we remove practical thinking altogether. We want to keep parochial ways of doing things, for these are the conditions for the possibility of innovation, personal flourishing, and the inception and development of art and culture. Group uniqueness is humanity's division of labour that allows for the emergence of various breakthroughs of practical wisdom. We need only look at the overcoming of tribalism in the interest of civil society, an insight that had first to occur as a local breakthrough before becoming a generally accepted political good.

Elimination of bias, then, is the removal of the common *non*sense without losing common sense intelligence itself. Let me suggest what seem to be the three most basic ways that practical intelligence can deal with the problem of bias: self-critical self-awareness; compensation for bias via rational control of 'appearances'; and compensation for bias in gradual increments rather than through radical change.

First, perhaps the most basic condition for overcoming group bias is a self-critical self-awareness, a common sense insight that would see the practically wise value of the harmonious integration of individuals, groups, and modes of thinking.[40] The most basic concern of any group is its own safety and well-being, and the ultimate safety and well-being would be realized in a world in which one knows that harmony, not enmity, exists between all persons and groups. The totalitarian move of eliminating group distinctions altogether is no longer a practical option, and the subjugation of all groups by the most powerful is only the recipe for sudden reversals of the same kind. Thus, real practical security is in the harmonious coexistence of various groups, and this requires some form of higher order insight that grasps the principles of integration, equity, and justice that would undergird such an ideal social order. My point here is to indicate that some higher social integration beyond 'our way of doing things' must become a *pragmatic* plank in 'our' platform. There is no reason that concrete and particular common sense insights cannot reflect upon their own logic and see the practicality of world federalism, for instance.

Thus, the basic tool for overcoming group bias is not self-criticism from some 'already known to be objectively true' socio-political theory (for theory is precisely what group bias cannot cope with) but the insight that one's own good is tied up ultimately with the good of all others, and that not all of my personal good can be attained in practicality itself. Moreover, insights into the similarity of our shared humanity undergird the sympathy and compassion that Nussbaum calls for in the first part of her theory of political morality.[41]

A second way to deal with the problem of bias is to compensate via a rational control of 'appearances.' Whatever benefits may result from attempts to compensate for dramatic bias, these will not result in its elimination because the problem lies at a level partly inaccessible to conscious and deliberate effort. Final bias elimination is a project too great for social engineering alone. The error to avoid here is the notion that correction for bias equals the elimination of bias. For the means we will choose to compensate for our biases are just as likely themselves to be alternative biases.

Nevertheless, there may be a place for wisely administered compensation. Given the cognitive principle of insight into *phantasm*, the furniture of the phenomenal field is no small contributor to insight induction. Thus the deliberate shaping of appearances, say, in technical symbols and schematics, enables insights to occur that were difficult or impossible without the new device. For instance, the insights of calculus ultimately rest upon insight into special notations rather than insight into counting pebbles. Thus, we can indirectly compensate for bias when we identify an impeding feature in appearances or when we create artificial appearances that may enable us to expand our viewpoint or experience base. This has been the purpose behind the reasonable form of affirmative action and may require more than one generation to accomplish. In the past, for example, no post office would ever hire a woman as a letter carrier because ... well, who ever heard of such a thing?! After a time of deliberate hiring of women, however, the notion of such prohibition simply ceases to arise because new appearances disallow that negative insight. Such incremental yet deliberate and responsible changes to appearances permit social progress precisely by working in congruence with the principle of our cognitive method, rather than at cross-purposes through coercion or censorship.

A third point about compensating for bias is that it must proceed gradually, precisely because it can enflame the emotions that are the problem here. For the very nature of practical and concrete intelligence is that it preserves successful insight and is very conservative regarding anything that might dislodge proven past success. Thus common sense has a suspicion of sudden or dramatic change, and tends to greet it with fear and resistance. As well, there is always the temptation to 'leave well enough alone' and accept the status quo. Yet as we have seen, there is a practical way to finesse changes to a group's common sense insight set and its attached biases. Herein lies the real art of politics.

Still, we are left with the problem of the unconscious emotional commitments of dramatic bias that all of us harbour as a result of our birth into and membership in some form of human grouping. How is this problem to be dealt with?

We would not want to eliminate emotion itself, for emotion per se is not error, and some emotion is absolutely necessary for moral and evaluative discernment. Yet emotion is at the root of salience pre-selection and this salience selection was deeply implanted in us before we had the critical capacity to screen and choose for ourselves. Neither is the formula we seek one of simply removing 'negative' emotion, for fear, anger, hate, and the like all have their place; one needs only to fear, hate, and be angry at the right objects, in the right way, to the right degree, at the right time, and so forth. The question we must answer, then, can take these three forms: Is there an emotion that correlates all other emotions in such a way as to function primordially as a salience selector while guaranteeing the avoidance or lessening of bias distortion? Can we learn to feel aright such that appearances will be construed towards an unhampered induction of the human good? Can such an emotion be stable enough to ground a way of life, say, a life devoted to *eudaimonia*?

Another Look at Patterns of Experience and Salience Selection

Even if we were able somehow to eliminate bias, patterns of experience are another matter. They are not the sorts of things that can or should be eliminated, nor is there a compensation that does not end up simply being a shift from one pattern to another. If consciousness is slippery, disallowing us to lock in place the desired mode of awareness, how can we maintain something like a steady state of 'being objective' in our moral cognition?

In my previous example of patterns of experience, I sketched the various ways that salience networks can emerge and shift, depending upon the fundamental concern dominating us at any given time. But this is not a doctrine held by Lonergan alone. Here is Nussbaum on the role of emotion in this regard:

> The child ... [in her development] has many emotions: joy at the presence of good things and fear of their absence; anger at the sources of frustration and gratitude for aid and comfort; shame at her inability to control the sources of good; envy of competitors and guilt at her own aggression; disgust at the slimy and the decaying; wonder at the beauty of the world. By now we can see how these emotions support the child's ability to act, as they *mark off patterns of salience and urgency in her surroundings*; we also see how they may support generous and beneficial action. (italics mine)[42]

Emotions illuminate salience, and our reading of Nussbaum told us why: emotions always involve an appraisal of something's close yet vulnerable connectedness to our eudaimonic sense of well-being. We don't get emotional unless we 'take things personally.' Lonergan's contribution here is to show that the many ways we do actually experience salience networks can be grouped into a small number of categorical ways of intending. For salience can be illuminated by emotions that themselves are guided by the most basic concerns: biological, aesthetic, intellectual, and dramatic.[43] Each of these general patterns of experience can be the backdrop for a variety of different emotive episodes; for example, the biological pattern of experience can incite fear, exhilaration, joy, frustration, as indeed can the aesthetic and the dramatic. Even intense intellectual concentration can involve emotions of anticipation, frustration, and the joy of discovery. Thus, we must distinguish between the salience provided by an emotional episode from the overall salience network that establishes the parameters of what one will emote about in the first place. In fact, this allows us to interpret emotions more accurately, for the fear one feels in the 'fight or flight' syndrome cannot have quite the same meaning as the fear one feels while watching a Greek tragedy on stage. The pattern of experience within which emotions occur is a vital part of our interpretive and evaluative criterion for the understanding of that emotion.

While I stated in chapter 3 that it is the dramatic pattern of experience, the one concerned with successful unfolding of concrete personal living that is the default centre from which life is lived, and hence the one most suited for living out the practically wise life, it would still be wrong to state that only that pattern can count as the right mode of ethical consciousness. For there is a human good proper to each pattern of experience: the biological pattern is ordered to physical well-being; the aesthetic to psychic and emotional well-being; the intellectual pattern to the attainment of the true and the real, and the dramatic pattern to the art of actually living well. All these are ways in which concerns that shape our patterns of salience can combine and differentiate in the attainment of the various aspects of the human good. The term *good* can be validly predicated across any of the patterns of experience, for each is a mode of being conscious of concerns that impinge upon the well-being of human nature.[44]

Therefore, the shifting nature of our patterns of experience need not block our pursuit of the good. Rather, in pursuing the human good we will naturally shift patterns as we seek to collect and balance the various goods that make up *eudaimonia.* Now this is not some new insight into how *phronesis* would work. For clearly the *phronimos* knows that when courageous combat is called for he will shift to the biological pattern of 'fight or flight,' and when contemplation is called for he will enter the intellectual or religious pattern of experience. The point is that each pattern may be rationally and responsibly allowed to obtain, and that each one can be moderated in balance with other pursuits (and their salience patterns), as governed by the overall life view best seen from the dramatic centre. Furthermore, the fruit of each pattern, such as new insights into ethics, can now join other elements available for wise integration by practical wisdom.

The Horizon of Concern, Emotion, and Patterned Experience

The other notion discussed in chapter 3 was the horizon of concern. Now each pattern of experience, with the exception of the intellectual pattern,[45] has its own limitation of interest that is indeed a kind of horizon, for the concerns one has while in the act of high-speed downhill skiing (biological survival, aesthetic delight) will probably utterly preclude any thought of, say, the periodic table of elements. But these salience-determining phenomenal fields are not the same as the one overall horizon of concern as Lonergan defines it.[46] For while we may slide from one pattern of experience into the next, the totality of interests across all our possible patterns is also limited to the questions and concerns we are *capable* of raising in the first place. Theoretically speaking, human intellect may have the potential for unlimited inquiry about the totality of being but in our actual lives, each of us only ever asks the questions that our temporally and historically contextualized concerns will permit. For just as we no longer ask mythological questions regarding which god is behind today's weather, but rather ask about air pressure and moisture conditions, so we do not know how to ask whole categories of questions that may become commonplace a thousand years from now. Our horizon of concern is limited by the fact that we do not know what we do not know, and hence cannot care about such things.

But apart from such epistemic limitation, our horizon of concern is also delimited by an emotional operator: our fundamental cares.[47] 'Care' is more than mere intellectual interest. It is the personal connection of the individual to matters that impinge upon her well-being, to one degree or another. It seems to me that horizon-limiting cares and concerns are analogous to Nussbaum's background emotions, for both have an effect upon what we encounter phenomenally, both are not themselves necessarily conscious objects of thought, and both may open or close whole areas to our attention. An example of a background emotion that truncates our horizon is fear. We may deny that fear is impacting our cognition and decisions, and yet dread and anxiety may arise when we are confronted with the realization that unknown vistas of reality lie beyond our horizon, that it may be the case that all our categories are inadequate, or worse, are distorting preconceptions.[48] Simply to ask such critical questions is to raise the possibility of going beyond our limits, but the prospect is threatening, and the comfort of bias and undisturbed ignorance calls us back from the edge – deselecting from salience those *phantasma* that might raise disturbing questions. A background fear of the unknown or of change indicates that some emotional inertia is at play in fixing our horizons.

But we seek a positive case of background emotion, one that is beneficial to ethical insight induction. Is there, then, a healthy emotion that would predispose us towards an expanding horizon of concern in a way analogous, say, to the open-ended commitment of scientific enquiry? Is there an emotion that allows us to shift across various limited patterns of experience, yet without truncating our horizon of concern?

Love as a Ground for Procedural Objectivity

Lonergan's candidate for such a background control emotion is the open-ended altruism, the self-sacrificing love commonly called *charity*. His claim is that charitable love keeps the horizon of concern maximized even while the subject is operating in a dramatic (practical), even biological pattern of experience.[49] Charitable love embodies a concern for the genuine good, both for oneself and for others; it is the extension to fellow humans of the same intimate concern that is intrinsic to proper self-love.[50] For love, according to Lonergan, recognizes both our own neediness and desire for real value; it also recognizes other persons as values in and of themselves in a thoroughgoing Kantian sense.[51]

Nevertheless, I think Lonergan's discussions of love become cryptic as they move towards religious experience. While such a move may be perfectly valid, I think Lonergan's interest in remaining historically and pragmatically connected to the world would lead him to value an articulation of ethical emotion that emerges from concrete human nature and society. In other words, while we may occasionally be blessed with the insight and examples of saints, the hope is that most of us may still act according to pretty sound ethics even without divinely implanted 'unrestricted love.'[52] Lonergan must have recognized this in his deference to the particular insights of practical wisdom in *Method in Theology*.[53] There, he chooses as the standard of sound ethical judgment Aristotle's *phronimos* and not the saint, for the *phronimos* is oriented to *this* world, even though he may be hoping and believing (or not) in the next one. I do not think Lonergan's phenomenology of religious experience is wrong here, though I think we can find a background emotion that is not a substitute for love but a more pragmatic expression of it.

In this regard, once again we find a rich and useful discussion in Nussbaum's treatment of compassion and love as central to psychological, ethical, and political health. Most of the 750 pages of her book *Upheavals of Thought* pursue a study of conceptions and narratives of love as developed in the literature of Plato, Aristophanes, Augustine, Dante, the Brontë sisters, Proust, Whitman, Joyce, and others. Her study aims at discovering the role that a rightly conceived notion of love could play in practical ethics and polity. Here I cannot restate Nussbaum's huge exposition but instead will extract the essential parts of her conception of love and compassion.

Love as Compassion

Since according to Nussbaum no emotion is good per se, apart from what it affirms or denies,[54] there must be normative criteria that determine whether love has erred or not.[55] She develops her positive criteria in contrast to such negative characterizations of love's traits as envy, unbridled passion, unseemly neediness, or the otherworldliness of Platonic and Augustinian loves. The following principles emerge as the elements of a love that is 'getting it right': recognition of the unique individuality of persons; reciprocity in human relations; and mediation of mercy and justice through compassion.[56] Thus, regarding individuality Nussbaum comments that 'any view of love that is going to be ethically good in itself, or conduce to further social goods, should recognize and make central the fact that human beings are individuals ... [with] qualitative distinctness ... that each has just one life to live, that a person's own life is a very salient fact.'[57] On reciprocity, she stipulates that love 'make room for and support reciprocal relationships of concern in which people treat one another not just as things, but as agents and as ends.'[58] Love 'should make room for and support general social compassion. The compassion supported by love should be built upon reasonable accounts of the three [above] judgments ... concerning seriousness of various human predicaments, our responsibility for these predicaments, and of the proper extent of concern.'[59]

Nussbaum thinks that these criteria and this conception of love do no violence to Aristotle's notions of *philia* (love, friendship) and *eleos* (pity, or compassion as Nussbaum translates it).[60] Lonergan would concur with these intersubjective distinctions, for a person goes beyond the limitations of emotive self-absorption 'when he is in love, when the isolation of the individual is broken and he spontaneously functions not just for himself but for others as well.'[61] Moreover, for Lonergan it is love that can correct for biases and keep the salience of the various patterns of experience from working against our personal and social interests. For 'it is by charity that we can move into the practical pattern of experience *without contracting our horizon*' (italics mine).[62]

As a *background* emotion, what influence would love-as-compassion have upon *phantasm* and the moral perception of salience?

First, love need not be overtly felt for it to have an impact. For compassionate love as the background concern would continually affect the topography of *phantasm*, it would illuminate and prioritize intentional objects, and do so with reference to the intrinsic value of individual persons. This will not necessarily be experienced as a deliberate assessment of worth, but as 'interpretive seeing' that will simply forbid us to overlook the salience of another human life.

Second, this way of seeing others as intrinsic values need not become self-effacing (a temptation common in religious traditions). Concern for our own well-being need not differ in kind from the concern we direct towards others. Here, then, compassion would mean 'feeling towards others a care that one initially feels towards oneself.' For we learn compassion by discovering that others are like ourselves, and this presupposes an unlearned self-love that is the basis of a healthy pursuit of genuine goods as well as an analogous regard for others.[63]

Thus the logic of compassionate love is that it aims at *eudaimonia.* For compassion is just another mode of the desire for happiness; it is the aversion to *un*happiness, both in oneself and in the other person. And it binds one's own flourishing to the flourishing of others in a more directly personal way than would, say, the political interest in justice and the mutual instrumentality of peaceful economic order. Precisely by allowing the emotion of compassionate love to become our main social orientation, we are making the judgment that we ought to err on the side of vulnerability if others are not flourishing along with us.

In light of this, how then are we to understand Lonergan's claim that love is the orientation that will permit us to shift into the practical, dramatic pattern of experience without contracting our horizon of concern?[64] Certainly, he cannot mean that people in love are constantly thinking about their beloved during each shifting pattern of experience, for lovers still are able to focus upon other things, yet always with a background sense that something wonderful is in the air.[65] Consider this example. When we go downhill skiing, we deliberately put ourselves into the biological and aesthetic patterns of experience, for we enjoy the sheer thrill and danger of it. Yet why do we so often prefer to share such an experience with friends? Surely the definition of solipsism is the peak experience of slaloming to save one's life, and yet we plan to ski with friends, relishing the presence of each other's whooping and hollering. Since the peak experience is personal, we seem to be aiming at a future in which *we will have done what we did together.*[66] The actual experience of skiing is a contracted pattern of experience, but one with a concern that extends outward to such whole-life values as friendship and memories. So too the practical focus of common sense and the dramatic pattern may still be deployed with an ulterior sense of concern for others; that is, for a future where we will have pursued our own group concerns – yet together, as a good society. Compassionate love and group loyalty, therefore, are not mutually exclusive.

I realize that this treatment of love has made some sweeping claims. They are more substantially argued for in Nussbaum's and Lonergan's works. I have more or less stated the claim that compassionate love is the background emotion most conducive to affecting *phantasm* in a way that rightly connects the value of the subject and object. But the purpose of this chapter is to see how objectivity could be understood if it were to include emotions of deep personal concern.

Objections to Love as a Bias

Some objections could be raised here. On the one hand, is it not the case that love itself is perhaps one of the strongest forms of bias? Surely, love strongly predisposes my preferences towards the happiness and advantage of my close circle of family, friends, and other loves. On the other hand, need we think that a family-love type of bias is a bad thing? Do we even need objectivity here? The force of the objection seems to come from the strength of emotion we feel in intimate circles but which then suddenly drops off towards indifference as we move outward towards mere fellow humans, as it were. Would this not cause serious distortion of *phantasm*? I will limit my response to these objections to a consideration of the special love within families.[67]

My response requires that we distinguish between the kind of overtly felt emotion that one has towards family and the notion of a background love – Nussbaum's love-as-compassion, or Lonergan's love as maximal horizon of concern. In the end, family love may be a proper special interest nested within a general background love-as-concern/care.

It need not follow that a focus of intense emotion, such as family love, must be considered a bad form of bias. Certainly, on the basis of arguments presented earlier in this book, we understand that strong emotion or vested interest will affect the network of phenomenal salience. But I have argued that the goal of virtue (and of the objectivity I am espousing here) is not the elimination of pockets of special salience but the acquisition of the right *kind* and *degree* of salience, relative to the agent, that would foster *eudaimonia*. Thus, a special interest is not by that fact alone an improper interest. As with all critiques of a virtue ethics model, we must consider the larger context.

Family love is certainly a form of preference, and as Nussbaum points out, its felt intensity increases with proximity of the loved person to my own *eudaimonia*. The emotion is considered good when directed towards the right person, at the right time, to the right degree, expressed in the right manner, and so forth. Given our view of human nature at this point, we would be wrong in virtue ethics to *fail* to love our children or spouses or parents as is fitting, given their place in our lives. We would be wrong to love our hamster more than our mother, as stated above, and equally wrong to love them with the same kind of love. The rightness of the love is something apart from whether it is a preference of one person or persons over other people or groups.

Thus, bias elimination cannot mean a call for the unrealistic extension of familial love to the whole world. Being objective in virtue ethics cannot mean the elimination of preferences; objectivity is the unhindered openness to attaining the right preferences.

Furthermore, given the view that my *eudaimonia* relies, in part, upon living in a healthy society, and that healthy families require special attention and devotion, then *your* proper familial love of *your* family, and *my* love of *mine*, will be necessary for a good neighbourhood, village, polis, or culture. For we all need co-workers and friends and playmates for our children who are not neurotic, neglected, and desperately over-dependent, and these are just three of the myriad problems arising from loveless or dysfunctional families. Our own flourishing, and that of the ones we care most deeply about, requires the general emotional health of fellow citizens. This is perhaps the ground of the state's interest in a minimal level of family decency, the violation of which invites legal intervention. Thus, my alternate concern for the general good of the many can be fulfilled, in part, by my attending to the preferences proper to familial love. The social and the personal are not mutually exclusive here. Rather, the well-functioning of personal relations may be the basis of well-functioning societies in general.

This brings me to my second point of defense. The reason, ultimately, that background love and familial love need not clash is that they differ in kind. Unlike the tendency of familial love, background love-as-compassion is never an overt feeling.[68] That is what defines it as a background phenomenon. What we *do* experience consciously in the grips of a background emotion is a pattern of experience that illuminates, in this case for example, the salience of the flourishing of others. Simply walking down the street within a background concern of compassion puts me in a certain positive stance regarding an oncoming fellow citizen, an extremely subtle general acceptance and perhaps benevolence that is only clearly identified by the contrasting experience of its absence. For if my background emotion is self-preservation at all cost, viewing others defensively or purely as instruments may be the major pattern of salience, perhaps becoming so generic and subtle as to be almost impossible to detect, though it would affect all I do and see.

Background emotion does not have a proximity to my personal *eudaimonia* the way feelings about significant people do. It is a fundamental set of concerns, usually operative without our explicit awareness, and thus insightfully detected inversely by reflection upon the things it makes salient. Family love is overtly felt, susceptible to grand variations of intensity and duration, and directly discernible, without the need for reflection. Therefore, because family and background loves differ categorically, we need be no less compassionate in our background-love approach to the world for being especially emotively involved in our own deeper, personal relationships. Hence, family love need not be a negative form of bias, and we do not need to choose between personal love and some general love of humanity.

Another objection can arise. To avoid bias, why rely upon any emotion at all, when Lonergan claimed that a self-correcting process is already at play in sound cognitive process, the pure desire to know? As self-correcting, is not the pure desire to know sufficient to lead towards bias elimination and therefore promote objectivity in virtue ethics?

This objection can be answered with three points. First, the pure desire to know would perhaps be sufficient were virtue attainable through knowledge alone. But the final end for humans is an *activity* of the soul that involves right desire and emotion as well as knowledge. Knowing and acting differ in kind, not degree. There is, therefore, no continuum from knowing to doing; otherwise *akrasia*, a weakness by which we act against our better judgment, would not be such a thorny problem. Vital as the pure desire to know is for sound cognitive operation, at some point cognition must give way to, or be transcended by, action and the outward thrust of interpersonal relationships. Second, the pure desire to know is the primordial push behind all *cognitive* development, but it cannot be the primordial push behind all human action in general, for this, by definition, aims at the *summum bonum* of *eudaimonia*. While the human good includes knowing, it is more than knowing itself. The fullness of human living is perhaps driven by a 'pure desire for the genuine good'; the pure desire to know, then, would be only a constituent of this. Finally, the operation of the pure desire to know would result in my eventually coming to know that knowledge alone is not enough. I would learn that some background emotion that rightly construes *phantasm* is also a necessary part of attaining the human good. I have argued in this book that love-as-compassion is the best candidate for that job, but even if it were not, some other general background concern would play the part, and the pure desire to know would not stand alone.

Performative or Procedural Objectivity Revisited

Nussbaum has argued that no emotion can make us automatically see all the right and good choices to the extent that we could say that that emotion is good per se. But just as some emotions are almost always the embodiment of wrong judgments (envy, contempt, bodily disgust, primitive shame), so some emotions are most conducive to judging things aright. I am claiming that since emotions are only prima facie judgments, it is too strong a thing to say that the right emotion alone 'gets it right' (for then it would be a per se good), but that this one emotion – compassionate love – construes *phantasm* into the pattern of salience most conducive to sound moral insight. Surely, having compassion towards self and other will allow one simply to 'see' hamsters as less salient than human mothers.

Being objective, then, means being in a state most conducive to maximizing the probability of sound moral insight occurrences. This involves two aspects, both of which are activities of the soul. First, one must self-consciously and responsibly take hold of the multi-leveled cognitive method so as to be involved in a self-correcting, self-critical openness to judgment of the real and the true. Second, one must be in the grip of a background emotion of love-as-compassion, desiring the good for oneself as well as for others. For the background emotion of love-as-compassion will not make the choices of *phronesis* for us, but will affect the *phantasm* that *phronesis* must face, and affect it so that other people together with whom we must work out our *eudaimonia* will be seen as the intrinsic values that they are.

In the light of the foregoing, what would a Nussbaumian, Lonerganian *phronimos* be doing when getting it right in moral insight induction? To begin with, we can identify at least three potential roadblocks to performative objectivity. If we remove them, or if we progress along a vector that is continually overcoming them, both personally and socio-politically, we can say that we are 'being objective.'

First, we must be continually yielding to exigencies of the pure desire to know. This is not simply the call to avoid bias and violent emotion; that would be simplistic and too obvious. Being objective in the sense promoted by Lonergan requires an insight into how insight works, an insight into the fact that we do not just 'see' what is the case but must arrive at this insight indirectly through a valid judgment. In other words, we must become self-aware of how cognitive operations work within us and then reasonably and responsibly take hold of them and deploy them methodically.

Second, on the basis of this critical self-awareness of the levels of our cognitive apparatus, we may become aware of the reality and danger of bias and the need to rationally alter appearances to begin to counteract its effects. Such projects of altering *phantasm* may involve everything from simple personal honesty to widespread reorganization of whole cultural, educational, and social arrangements. There will be the need for practising the art of seeing things from the viewpoints of others. There will be needed the courage to face new possibilities presented through moral imagination. All these steps are the recognition that we must work within the constraints of emotional structures latent in our habits and customs, as well with as the emotional structure of our biases.

Third, therefore, the *phronimos* must also desire and feel aright, and here we are moving beyond a strict Aristotelian model when we call for the desires and feelings of love-as-compassion in ways that he did not do at all. Still, according to Nussbaum, this is not an addition to Aristotle that is particularly ill fitting. Rather, by becoming increasingly open to the presentations that would foster empathy leading to compassion, love can be said to aid, not hinder, our perceptions of value around us. How a society is to foster such open-ended love is beyond the scope of this book. Indeed, it seems that both Lonergan and Nussbaum think it is beyond the scope of philosophy itself.

In any case, if we are growing in the actuation of these three aspects of cognition and emotion, we will find ourselves in a constantly self-developing dynamic in which the probability of sound moral insight occurrence will be increasingly recognized and continually maximized. This is the definition of what I have called procedural objectivity. This has not solved the mystery of the emergence of sympathy and altruism any more than it has the mystery of induction. We may fail to understand their origins or even their inner workings, but we can advert to the reality and importance of their existence, and then intelligently, responsibly, and compassionately exploit the method that maximizes their occurrence.

Concluding Summary

My project in this book has been an examination of the subjective pole of the psychology and phenomenology of moral insight; that is, a look at practical wisdom from the driver's seat of the *phronimos.* Since the goal of Aristotle's virtue ethics was not to expound a theory of the good per se, but to explain to the well-prepared student the elements that go into living the good life, it has been worth looking at just what is going on from the point of view of the practitioner of *phronesis.* For the call is ultimately for readers of such an ethics to take what they can from it and apply it to the actual lives they are living. To that end, I have presented a subject-based description of the operations and experiences the agent will go through when engaging the various levels of practical insight. This too concerns making agents familiar with their own personal cognitive psychology in an effort to make recognizable new terrain and reaffirm familiar ones. Thus, I have avoided much metaethics and have tried to present a description and explanation of practical intelligence in action.

Lonergan's contribution to the project is a philosophical psychology that is ultimately grounded in a phenomenology of the conscious operations of the subject. Each reader of his work must confront the fact that he or she is being invited to verify the reality of the generalized empirical method. This will happen if readers attend to the data of their own consciousness, understand by insight the operations therein, and affirm that indeed they are operating (or not) in this manner. The act of wondering about the method ends up bringing the method into operation. Therefore, this empirical verification acts as an immanent and self-evident first principle at the foundation of both the reader's continued personal growth and of the argument in the rest of Lonergan's works.

The foundational nature of insight and the generalized empirical method that exploits it ground the subjective pole of a theory of procedural (or performative) objectivity. (The objective pole is grounded in the being of whatever is real, true, and good.) In addition to being self-evidently foundational, the method is also understood to be normative, for we know that we ought to be cycling through the various cognitive stages or else risk placing ourselves at the mercy of rashness and bad luck in our 'coming to know.' It is through awareness of the normative nature of this cognitive method that we see by contrast the characteristic dangers of the various modes of bias that infringe upon sound deployment.

Nussbaum's contribution has been in two main areas: the nature of 'appearances' and corresponding human action;[1] and the cognitive capacities of emotion, especially love. Her latest foray into literature, poetry, and music is a worthy pursuit in its own right and will perhaps lead to considerable enrichment in the philosophy of love. However, I have restricted myself simply to extracting the psychological aspects of her work in order to fill out Lonergan's account of emotive cognition. Nussbaum's work is rich enough to deserve far more attention, but my strategy of comparing Lonergan and Aristotle has required that I use her account of love's knowledge in what amounts to a supplementary fashion.

This is because Nussbaum's arguments regarding emotional intelligence leave out too much of the role of an overarching set of cognitive acts. Primarily, I think that her interest in revealing the intuitive nature of emotions has led her to invest them with too much, leaving out a sufficient account of reflective critical insight. Certainly animal emotion and animal motion do not operate with such reflection. But this is a large part of why animals do not share in *eudaimonia.* The specifically human aspect of *eudaimonia* is that it invites us to become conscious and deliberate partakers, to some degree, in the restructuring of our own natures, making of ourselves a work of art, as it were. This is not possible for us apart from forays into critical reflection.

My own contribution has been to use Nussbaum's and Lonergan's frameworks to articulate an activity called 'being objective' (performative or procedural objectivity) that counters another activity called 'being biased.' I have not attempted to develop a complete theory of moral objectivity, nor an exhaustive justification of moral truth claims. I have identified several weaknesses in a virtue ethics such as Aristotle's and have tried to show how many of the concerns associated with these weaknesses can be addressed. I have tried to stay closer to the subjective pole, describing the patterns, operations, and emotive vectors within which and through which we must all make our practical decisions.

Aristotle's ethics remains the exemplar of living life well. He presents a strong case for a holistic interaction between perception, desire, emotion, appearance, insight, judgment, deliberation and decision. These elements line up as the sequential parts of a dynamic cognitive method: *phronesis*. His treatment of *phronesis* as it stands in the texts does indeed leave some difficulties (for example, its ultimate connection with *nous* and *aisthesis*; and whether or not there really is something like the 'practical syllogism'). But he excels in bringing together two very disparate ends of the human ethical situation: the need for an openness to the contingencies of particular circumstances of particular agents, and the need for a robust theory of truth in ethics. Analogous to his correspondence theory of truth, this turns out to be truth in correspondence with right desire.[2] But the rightness of the desire is not the rightness of mere preference, but the rightness of a desire that longs for what is genuinely good for one's flourishing. Thus, Aristotle still presents a respectable and valid ethics, though one that will continue to evolve as our understanding of human nature and our precision of perceptive discrimination increases.

In the course of writing this book, I have personally experienced and verified many of the truths I have learned from Aristotle, Lonergan, and Nussbaum. Over and over again while reflecting upon their insights, I have been reminded that reading a treatise on ethics does not make one good or happy. Becoming a good human being is far more a matter of practice than knowledge. I have caught myself in a radical salience shift on more than one occasion, where a change in emotional predisposition seriously changed the appearance of things. This is especially true in reflecting upon the political and social events of the world. There is vital data for ethical decision making that is only detected when we take the time to put ourselves in another person's place, to listen to the unspoken narrative contained in the passion with which other people are responding to their circumstances, and to try to feel what they are feeling. Whatever cultural differences divide the world, joy is still joy, and misery is still misery. Only through exploring ways to expand our horizon of concern, to practise the art of deliberate caring and compassion for all comers will we discover in ourselves the perceptual acumen of love. And love is both an end in itself as well as the highest enabling means for living a good human life.

Notes

Introduction

1 *Phronimos*, used throughout as a substantive, is an adjective of two endings with both the masculine and the feminine singular ending in *–os*. It is, therefore, a suitable gender-neutral term, and I shall freely apply it to male and female moral experts without doing injustice to principles of grammar or equity. See Smyth 1956, sec. 288–9.

2 Dreyfus and Dreyfus 1990, 247–8; see also DesAutels 1996.

3 Simonton 1984.

4 See for example Zsambock and Klein 1997; Kaplan and Simon 1990; Gick and McGarry 1992.

5 Lonergan was educated at Heythrop College (University of London) and Gregorian University in Rome. His career included professorships at the Gregorianum (Rome), Regis College (University of Toronto), Harvard Divinity School, and Boston College. He produced works in economics, philosophy of history, philosophical psychology, epistemology, methodology, and theology. Among other distinctions, he was made a Companion of the Order of Canada and received honorary doctorates from twelve American and Canadian universities. Lonergan's work displays eclectic influences from Aquinas, Kant, Hegel, J.H. Newman, and Max Scheler, and integrates evolutionary theory, probability theories, and depth psychology. A short biography of Lonergan is found in Morelli and Morelli 1997, 4–25.

6 Lonergan 1971, 264–5.

Chapter 1

1 *Nicomachean Ethics*, Book X offers a discussion of pleasure and its relation to the conception of the final good for human beings. The project of this book,

however, is not overly concerned with conceptions of happiness, but focuses more on the aspects of cognition deployed in particularist ethical insight. Thus, while sidestepping the pleasure discussion in Book X, I will cover the topic as it emerges in the first three books – as a phenomenal pleasantness associated with intentional objects deemed good or desirable by us. A further topic of Book X – contemplation – introduces another mode and object of intelligence that, while fascinating in its own right and part of a deeper study of the final good, is not directly relevant to a theory of objectivity that is grounded in emotive intelligence. Also, it is not altogether clear that Book X's conception of happiness is consistent with the more earthly focus of the first part of the *Nicomachean Ethics* (henceforth *NE*), but such discussion is beyond to scope of this project.

2 Annas 1993, 27.

3 *NE* 1094b12–27; 1096b30–33.

4 *NE*, Bk I, ch. 1.

5 *NE* 1094a24.

6 *NE*, Bk I, ch. 4. Aristotle critiques the Platonic conception that the good is an eternal, unchanging Form, and all lesser, human goods are caused to be good through their participation in that ideal Form. His criticism is essentially twofold. First, this view of the good cannot account for the apparent incommensurability of the actual goods we pursue; and second, an ideal Form of the good is simply not something attainable for humans anyway. The first criticism reduces to the problem inherent in treating the good as belonging to a high category, when it does not; or again, of predicating the good across categories as if it were an identical attribute in all of them. Clearly, this is not the case. 'Good' has as many senses as, say, 'being' and as such can be predicated only analogically across many distinct categories. There is a good applicable to substance, to quality, to quantity, to relation, to time, and to place. It cannot be present in the same way in all these categories, yet a universal good must be predicated in the same way of all it subjects. Further, if the good were an identical attribute predicable to all its specific sub-categories, a single science (*episteme*) would derive from it. But medicine, gymnastics, and strategy all participate in the good, yet there is no single science that comprehends them all. The 'good' is simply not some common element answering to one Form. If this is so, the goods are not commensurate upon a single scale of any kind, and we must treat the notion very differently than we would treat a generic first principle that might ground a single science.

The second criticism is terse but relevant. Even if the good were an eternal, independently subsisting Form, it would for that very reason *not* be what we are looking for. We seek the good for *us*, for us *as* humans; human action is aimed at a good that is achievable for humans. Otherwise, it could not be defined as the 'human good.' *NE*, Bk I, ch. 6.

7 *NE* 1097a19–b7.

8 *NE*, Bk I, ch. 7.

9 *NE* 1097b23–1098a3. An interesting essay on this subject that uncovers ambiguities in the intellectualist interpretation of human function is Nagel 1972.

10 *NE* 1099a7–8.
11 *NE* 1101a14–17.
12 Clearly, no single English word satisfactorily conveys all these notions: 'happiness' certainly does not, for it connotes the idea of a present, experiential, and psychological enjoyment. But as we have seen so far, Aristotle's term *eudaimonia* is a much more complex notion. Throughout this book, I will use the Greek term *eudaimonia* as the final good for humans. I do this to put some distance between Aristotle's concept and our propensity to make subjective enjoyment too central a notion. As well, *eudaimonia* has become a technical term largely acceptable in its own right in the discourse of philosophical ethics.
13 *NE* 1102b30–1103a1.
14 *NE* 1103a6–10.
15 The term 'ought' must remain indeterminate until we discuss that standard by which the practically wise person would resolve it.
16 *NE*, Bk II, ch. 1.
17 *NE* 1103a23–25.
18 *NE*, Bk II, ch. 2.
19 *NE* 1103b31–33; also *NE*, Bk VI, ch. 13.
20 *NE* 1103b26–1104a9.
21 *NE* 1104b4–13.
22 *NE*, Bk II, ch. 5.
23 Irwin's translation (1985) is interesting: 'Virtue, then, is (a) a state that decides, (b) [consisting] in a mean, (c) the mean relative to us, (d) which is defined by reference to reason, (e) i.e., to the reason by reference to which the [*phronimos*] would define it. It is a mean between two vices, one of excess and one of deficiency.' *NE* 1106b35–1107a4.
24 *NE* 1105a27–1105b19.
25 *NE*, Bk III, ch.1.
26 *NE* 1111b4–1112a13.
27 *NE* 1111b20–27, 1112a19ff.; *De Anima* (henceforth *DA*) 433b27ff.
28 *NE* 1113a13.
29 Character is not totally determinative of such ethical perception, for even with bad habits one can wonder about and infer ends other than those already integrated into one's character. And this can be going on in an *un*reflective manner – one can acquire ends unconsciously, by habit, by imitation, by emotion, or by experience. 'Comfortable directions [are chosen because they] represent unconscious analogues of conscious attempts to bring one's desires and dispositions [into] accord with a reflective inductive judgment about what one ought to be doing' (Dahl 1984, 49).
30 This merger of perception and evaluation or judgment is worked extensively throughout Nussbaum 1986 and 2001.
31 *NE* 1139a25.
32 *NE* 1139a30.
33 *Phronesis* can be distinguished by contrasting it with other Greek modes of intellectual operation. *Episteme* concerns the theoretical and not the practi-

cal, while *techne, sunesis,* and *gnome* do not issue in prescription. *Poiesis* may prescribe, but its injunctions concern objects external to us, and hence not directly relevant to *praxis. Nous* is actually a more complicated issue to be dealt with later.

34 *NE* 1140b20–21.

35 *NE* 1141b4–23.

36 *NE* 1142a12–19.

37 *NE* 1142a15; also 1143a25–b14.

38 *NE* 1142a20–31.

39 *NE* 1144a28–35.

40 *NE* 1144b30–33.

41 *NE* 1095b4–14.

42 See further nuances on this point in McDowell 1996, 31–2; also Burnyeat's well-known work 'Aristotle on Learning to be Good' (1980).

43 Jaeger, after etymological study of *kalokagathia,* describes the person of virtuous disposition as 'practicing his vocation with real pleasure and full understanding, [having] his heart in the right place' (Jaeger 1939, 175).

44 The term 'practical particularism' refers to an ethics that will not decide moral issues apart from references to actual circumstances that elicit moral inquiry. In general, particularism does not reject moral rules, but understands them to function more as guidelines than as universal maxims. Particularism allows mitigating circumstances to amend rules of thumb; as such, particularism operates and develops analogously to the common law. An excellent pro and con discussion regarding particularist theories is found in Hooker and Little 2000.

45 Nussbaum herself has recanted some parts of her earlier view of the nature of *phantasm* and animal motion, adding enough clarifications to eliminate Wedin's criticisms of her. See Nussbaum 1986, xx. Wedin 1988, 90–9, takes issue with Nussbaum; Richardson 1992, 385, n. 12 corrects Wedin.

46 *DA* 431a7–9: *hoion kataphasa e apophasa,* 'a kind of affirmation or denial' (Hett 1936 trans.); 'a quasi-affirmation or denial' (McKeon 1941 trans.).

47 I am not saying that *nous* and *phronesis* are unable to apprehend value. I am saying that emotions may apprehend the same values that intellect may apprehend, but in a way that may affect our phenomenal construal of the world differently.

48 *NE* 1139a21.

49 This response is quite distinct from a Humean belief/desire combination. That account conceives emotions as conveying no cognitive content at all, but supplying the 'pushy state' towards or away from a content provided by belief (see Dancy 1991, 414–15). It is clear from Aristotle's presentation that the trainable parts of the desires are those that share in thought to some degree. The desires always long for what appears pleasant and fine and flee from the opposite. The key to moral maturity is for the desires to begin to find attractive the *genuine* human good, and this means learning, by habituation, the actual beauty of the good. In Humean models of motivation, the desires are in principle not trainable; they are, as Nussbaum puts it, 'hard-

wired in psychology, lacking in intentionality and impervious to modification' (2001, 136). In contrast, for Aristotle they are partly cognitive and are justifying insofar as their unique form of cognition can be said to attain truth.

50 See *Rhetorica* 1378a30–b9, where a situation of intense anger provides a source of pleasure – the pleasure of imagining (*phantasia*) acts of revenge; and 1385b12–1386a3, where Aristotle describes appearances designed to evoke pity; also, all of Book II, ch. 6 on shame and shamelessness. These texts are impossible to read without our imaginations evoking scenes of complex human interactions and predicaments. Aristotle's full awareness of the emotional evaluations of these situations grounds his use of them in the art of persuasion (beliefs, affirmations, judgments). If orectic responses of pursuit or avoidance were not a mode of judgment, at least regarding values and the good, they could not play the role they do in the *Rhetoric.* Of course, it is precisely because emotional judgment is only of things 'as they appear' that it is extremely vulnerable to the deception of unethical rhetoricians. For good additional discussion see Striker 1996.

51 *NE* 1105b26; cf. 1105b21–1106a13, 1109a23. See Sherman 1989, 165–71; Leighton 1982.

52 *NE* 1114b1ff.

53 I rely in this section upon Frede 1992; also Sherman 1989, 59ff; Nussbaum 1994, ch. 3, and 1978, essay 5. Philippe 1971 provides a good essay on *phantasia* in Aristotle.

54 I am not going to discuss the aspect of this terminology that relates *phainomena* to *endoxa* (opinion). The term can be translated to mean a kind of prevalent opinion held by many. This usage is what Nussbaum refers to when analysing Aristotle's dialectical and empirical method used in the *Nicomachean Ethics.* See *NE* 1145b1ff; and detailed discussion in Nussbaum 1986, ch. 8.

55 Brentano 1969, 68–9.

56 *DA* 424a17.

57 See Frede 1992, 284–5. Note that after-images are not ascribed to memory because they are the lingering appearance of something *as though still present,* as when I retain a sense of the bottom floor of the house I am viewing while scanning the top level. Memory, on the other hand, according to Aristotle's definition, is precisely to remember the past *as* past. *Phantasm* 'remembers,' as it were, the image as still present. *De Memoria* 450a21ff.

58 Indeed, Aristotle places *phantasia* under the rubric of *kritika,* thus identifying it with some mode of critical discernment. This is the first sense of *phantasia* described by Aristotle in the beginning of *DA* Bk III, ch. 3, before 428a1, as 'an interpretive mental act in connection with perception.' Thus, this final sense of the term *phantasia* relates to the power to interpret perceptions, to make judgments or distinctions, especially by using comparative imaging. See Hankinson 1990.

59 *DA* 427b15, 25.

60 *DA* 430a31–b5; cf. 426b22, 31 and 427a9.

61 *DA* 431b12ff; for Aristotle's 'snub-nose' example, see *Metaphysics,* Bk VII, ch. 5.

62 *DA* 433b2, 28.
63 Frede 1992, 288–9. She is referring to *DA* 431a14–17, 433b12–28.
64 *DA* 434a5–7; *Historia Animalium* 542a30–2.
65 *DA* 434a10.
66 Richardson 1992, 385.
67 Ibid.
68 *DA* 428b10–17.
69 Wedin 1988, 249; Nussbaum 1978, 266.
70 Wedin says, 'To think of a proposition involves something like a sentential [re]presentation of that proposition. Indeed, if *De Anima* III.10's calculative imagination (*logistike phantasia*) can be made to cover pictorial [re]presentations, then one kind of *phantasma* might be something like a sentence token' (1988, 249).
71 This is very important for three reasons. First, it reminds us that visual *phantasms* are not at all the only form of phenomenal presentation: aural (spoken word), tactile (as in the case of Helen Keller, discussed in the next chapter), and other sense modes may provide the presentations of abstract thought. We must be careful to avoid obsessing on visual analogies, for these strongly prejudice us in favour of pictorialism. Second, I think that allowing for a descriptionalist theory of cognition is really the only way to construct the complex *phantasms* requisite for narratives and story-like case studies used in ethical description and reflection. Third, pictorialist notions of *phantasm*, requiring a strong similarity between mental images and their content, make it very difficult to see what a 'moral' *phantasm* would look like, for the good is not some discrete sensible feature supervening upon sensible objects and their representations. The good, if not abstract, is a trans-categorical incommensurate predicate that would not be captured adequately by an actual aspect of some one sense mode. This is just another reason for rejecting an intuitionist model of moral insight along the lines of Moore 1903. A good treatment of pictorialism versus descriptionalism is found in Tye 1991.
72 *NE*, Bk III, ch. 1.
73 Wedin says in this regard, 'Although images may be required as [re]presentational devices, we have seen that they do not in their own right have the required semantic property of aboutness. Only in the context of thinking about an object can it be meaningfully asked what the involved image is an image of. Aboutness is a feature of the complete intentional act, not of the [re]presentational structure involved in the act. So the requirement of similarity cannot have semantical force' (1988, 249).
74 Nussbaum 1986, 315.
75 *NE* 1110a4ff.
76 Nussbaum 1986, 312–13.
77 Nussbaum 1990 and 2001.
78 Sherman claims that she differs from Nussbaum and others by placing a greater emphasis on future intentions in the deliberative and decision process (1989, 57–60).
79 Ibid., 35–6.

80 Thus, a person who is wise regarding her own choices is Aristotle's fine and decent judge of other's actions. See *NE* 1143a25–31.
81 Sherman 1989, 42.
82 *NE* 1114b1ff.
83 A nice discussion of friendship as a moral mirror by which we gain self-knowledge is in Sherman 1989, ch. 4, especially pp. 141–4. She distils arguments from *NE* Bk IX, ch. 9; *Eudemian Ethics* Bk VII, ch. 12; and *Magna Moralia* Bk II, ch. 15.
84 *NE* 1169b33; *Magna Moralia* 1213a12–25.
85 I am following Wiggins 1978. Similar interpretations are presented in Dunne 1993 and in Byrne 1997, 63–78.
86 The role of *nous* in grasping ends is treated shortly.
87 *NE* 1098b3–4.
88 'Prejudged' is not to say 'prejudiced' or falsely construed. If we allow that our moral teachers have instilled in us the right objects of desire and the right habits, then these are accepted *as right* by the docile student prior to being personally verified as right by later mature reflection and experience. The moral world is prejudged for us by the judgment of our teachers and their experience. We receive these judgments through trust, and we do this precisely so that the phenomenal world we face as ethical neophytes will start out rightly construed. Moral development does not try to eliminate phenomenal construal, it tries to acquire and hone 'right construal' so that what really is good will seems so as well. See Burnyeat 1980.
89 *NE* 1142a14–15. The standard background on perception, memory, and experience is in *Metaphysics* Bk I, ch. 1, and *Posterior Analytics* Bk II, ch. 19.
90 *NE* 1179b20–31.
91 *NE* 1180a31.
92 *NE* 1180b6.
93 *NE* 1169b33–1170a3; cf. *NE* 1157b30–35.
94 Cf. *NE* 1179b32–35.
95 *NE* 1109b23, 1143b11–14, 1144b8–13.
96 This calls for a decision process able to account for redeployment of values and ideals in new situations, and new understandings of old ones. Such a decision process would have to involve a dialectical dynamic by which unsatisfactory options may cause the agent to refer back to the original concerns and re-evaluate them in the light of the means available. This dialectical conception is found in Wiggins 1978, 147.
97 Gomez-Lobo 1995, 27.
98 *NE* 1142a23–30.
99 Another view is that the triangle is seen as the primary figure necessary for the construction of a more complex geometric one.
100 Sherman 1997, 257. She is explicitly indebted to Dancy 1993 for the notion of 'shape' of circumstances.
101 Wiggins 1978.
102 Ibid., 145.
103 Ibid., 146.

104 My adaptation of the translation of *NE* 1143a32ff. in Wiggins 1978.
105 Term from Wiggins 1978.
106 Ibid.; parentheses mine.
107 DeMoss 1990 presents well the case for seeing something as instrumental.
108 The standard discussion of the practical syllogism is found in Allan 1955.
109 Wiggins 1978, 146–7. John McDowell approaches in a more phenomenological manner the notion of practical syllogism: the major premise is a general conception of how to live but not concretely spelled out in universal terms (be noble, be just, etc.). Rather, the major premise is manifest as the very set of real concerns evoked by encountered circumstances; the minor premise is the situational appreciation that the *phronimos* brings to bear on these circumstances. See McDowell 1979.
110 *NE* 1144a21–29.
111 Robert Louden provides this interpretation on the role given to *nous* in the following passage: 'When Aristotle asserts that *phronesis* is *nous,* he means two things: that the practically wise man is able non-inferentially to grasp the first principles of practical philosophy. But again, the former use is dominantly in the practical writings, since here we are concerned with action, and action concerns particulars. The epistemic drive is primarily towards particulars in the practical sciences; towards universals in the theoretical. And the intuitive capacities that Aristotle refers to when he employs *nous* in its epistemic senses are not (Engberg-Pedersen to the contrary) "mysterious." He is simply pointing to two well-established limits of inference, and asserting that *phronesis* must include more than knowledge by inference. This is not, of course, to say that *phronesis* is only *nous.* Practical wisdom also involves deliberation, which does entail inferential reasoning' (Louden 1986, 134).
112 See Sherman 1997, 244ff.
113 Equity as relying upon the perceptions of justice is discussed in Aristotle's *NE,* Bk V, ch.10. Sherman 1989, 13ff. has some discussion on this.
114 Sherman 1987, 244. Irwin 2000, however, claims that Aristotle's deference to 'theoretically significant generalizations' means he is not at all a particularist. But I think this is mistaken, for some sort of particularist claim still holds as long as two conditions are met: (i) that a thing or reason for action that was salient in one case may not be salient in another case of the same general kind; and (ii) that it is the wise eye of the *phronimos* that determines this. With *eudaimonia* as a controlling general notion and wise concrete insight as part of what constitutes it, a 'qualified' particularism is a valid term for Aristotelian ethical procedure.
115 Nussbaum 1986, 316.
116 Sherman 1997, 245.
117 Though I am in agreement with Wiggins and Sherman on these matters, other scholars think a covert insight into some universal or general good is intrinsic to *phronesis.* For Engberg-Pedersen, it is the universals discerned in the particulars that *phronesis* confronts (1983, 207 and 211). Sorabji argues that the *phronimos* has a 'general view of the good life' that, along with habituated right desires, induces insight into the particulars of moral deliberation

(1980, 206–7). Dahl thinks objectivity derives from the rationality of the deliberative process: critical reflection uncovers ends and motives that are truly what one was seeking through the discernment of moral habituation (1984, 21, 48–60). The enquiry of ethics brings to light the universals implicit in the habits of the *phronimos.* Cooper disconnects syllogistic reasoning from the final ethical insight by separating the inferential aspect (the moral syllogism) from the perception of particulars (1975, 19–21, 44). Deliberation determines inferentially the *kinds* of things to be done or sought, while direct perception picks out suitable *instances* of these kinds. See also Walsh 1999.

118 *NE* 1113a32–33.

119 *NE* 1107a29–32.

120 *NE* 1143b4–5. In regard to this, Louden sums up nicely ideas that are shared by Sherman and Nussbaum: 'Trustworthy moral principles can generally only be found by a dialectical process which starts from particular moral judgments and builds upwards. The practically wise man's intuition about what he should do in a particular situation is generalized in a maxim that applies to other agents in similar situations' (Louden 1986, 135). The other commentators would add, 'But they apply only as rules of thumb.' This is echoed in Burnyeat 1980, 72–3.

121 *NE* 1140b12–19, 1113a23–b1, 1114a3ff.

122 *NE* 1139a21–27, 1105b6–9.

123 *NE* 1107a1–3, 1176a3–29.

124 There is considerable disagreement among scholars regarding the degree to which Aristotle is involved in a vicious circle on this point. Monan, for instance, claims that the obvious interpretation of Aristotle here is that his argument is circular, for practical wisdom ultimately gets defined by reference to itself (1968, 83–4). Greenwood (1909, 157) and Gauthier and Jolif (1970, 2:435) also think circularity is inescapable. Mackie (1977, 186) agrees, charging that Aristotle's view on the good life and how we go about deciding what to do 'is too circular to be very helpful.' Grote (1890, 515–17), on the other hand, calls it an *apparent* circularity, an *apparent* incongruity. Ackrill (1973, 24; 1981, 138) thinks the key texts are obscure but that the putative account that charges circularity is probably incorrect. Dahl (1984, 65) and Cooper (1975) also grapple with apparent circularity and offer various ways out of the problem. We can see, then, that while there are exegetical difficulties in Aristotle, the circularity problem seems to arise from the general theory itself. A helpful article addressing this issue is Peterson 1992.

Chapter 2

1 Sternberg and Davidson 1995, 38.

2 Wallace 1991, 41–2.

3 Friedrich August von Kekule dreamed of whirling snakes that revealed to him the structure of benzene – the organic chemical compound making up of a ring of carbon atoms. He reported the dream many years after it took place, in a speech at a dinner commemorating his discovery: 'I turned my

chair to the fire [after having worked on the problem for some time] and dozed. Again the atoms were gamboling before my eyes. This time the smaller groups kept modestly to the background. My mental eye, rendered more acute by repeated vision of this kind, could now distinguish larger structures, of manifold conformation; long rows, sometimes more closely fitted together; all twining and twisting in snakelike motion. But look! What was that? One of the snakes had seized hold of its own tail, and the form whirled mockingly before my eyes. As if by a flash of lighting I awoke ... Let us learn to dream, gentlemen.' From Weisberg 1992, 86. The cases of Poincaré and Einstein are described in Gruber 1995.

4 Schooler et al. 1993, cited in Sternberg and Davidson 1995, 559–87.

5 Ibid., 570.

6 See Poincaré 1952, 52–4.

7 Recounted in Vitruvius 1914.

8 Sternberg and Davidson 1995, chs. 11 and 16.

9 Ibid., 449.

10 Schooler et al. 1993, cited in ibid., 576.

11 Lonergan 1992, 28–31.

12 For more on conditions of insight induction see the works of Gick and McGarry 1992; Kaplan and Simon 1990; and Dreyfus and Dreyfus 1990.

13 Lonergan 1992, 303.

14 Lonergan 1992, 37–43; but see the many index entries under 'Development.'

15 The generalized empirical method is the recognition that the hypothetico-deductive method, whose example par excellence is modern empirical science, is also operative in analogous forms across all other projects of enquiry. This conception of method will be further developed in the course of this project. See the 'canon of operations' in Lonergan 1971, ch. 1; 1993, 142–3.

16 I use the term 'coming to know' for its participial force – it is an ongoing process. To refer to human knowledge as an accomplished state is already to downplay somewhat the procedures that necessarily precede it and that will use one level of knowledge as the foundation for future development. Thus throughout this inquiry, I will refer to human knowing as process, as something we do. This is not to deny that the process has a product – the various blocks of propositional or habitual knowledge found in, say, concept and skill, books and arts. But the product depends upon the operations, and the operations depend upon conscious subjects performing them.

17 I deliberately begin with the case of Helen Keller to avoid emphasizing insight into *visual* data. It is too easy to confuse visual recognition with insight itself. Even the term 'insight' banks on an analogy to vision that is as potentially misleading as it might be illuminating. We learn so much of what we know through vision that we may tend to construe human cognition by analogy to vision; that is, to construe knowing as intuition, similar to sense intuitions. This is an area of one of Lonergan's most virulent critiques: knowing is not like 'taking a good look' at what is out there to be known. He combats such intuitionism along with its epistemological correlates in naive realism in

Lonergan 1992, 410–11, 437–40. (For an important critique of Duns Scotus's view that we directly intuit a nexus of conceptual content, see Lonergan 1997, 39, n. 126; a critique of scholastic conceptualism as well as Kant in this regard is in Lonergan 1968, 8–19.

18 Keller 1904.

19 Lonergan includes within the category of conscious data not only the various modes of sensible presentation, but also awareness of emotions, bodily sensations, and awareness of (some) mental acts.

20 Of the many things that can be said of the psychological phenomenon of attention, the most important for this study is the distinction and function of two kinds of awareness best described in Polanyi 1958. There are two major kinds of attention: focal attention and subsidiary attention. For example, in playing the piano, I can focus attention upon the music and the notation while also being conscious of the fact that my hands and fingers are moving and feeling too. The awareness of hand motion is subsidiary to the focused attention of musical notation. These are not levels or degrees of one general act of attention, but two distinct kinds of awareness, for one cannot slide along an unbroken continuum of focus without losing sight of what one was doing. When the pianist, for instance, shifts attention from the music being played to what his fingers are doing, he often gets confused and has to stop. This illustrates that the act of playing music is not the same as the act of the fingers, though it is built upon them. Fingering skill is the subsidiary material of the art of musicianship. Attention is not something that we merely shift from the music to the fingering. Rather, one can only focus attention on one level at one time. Another analogy is the relationship of words and sentences. One can focus either on each word and its connotations and denotations, or one can focus upon the meaning of the entire sentence, but not at the same time and in the same way. As Polanyi says, 'All the particulars become meaningless if we lose sight of the pattern which they conjointly constitute' (1958, 57). This two-level mode of attention – to that which is in focus, and yet still with a subsidiary but weaker awareness of constitutive element of focused objects – allows one to move upward, as it were, to higher order viewpoints of focus that permit of a gestalt-like grasp of wholes that was unavailable on the lower level. Lonergan builds a considerable amount of his theory of perception and insight on this kind of hierarchy of levels of attention and the corresponding higher order insight that each level may induce. Lonergan's theory will become clearer as we proceed.

21 Judgment is used here to denote existential judgment, or judgment of truth or falsity. Throughout, following Lonergan, I use the term judgment as assent to truth or being. I never use it in reference to the act of composition and division, or the attribution of a predicate to a subject; these are discursive acts of the understanding by which we grasp the nature of complex objects of thought – first order insights of understanding. 'Judgment' is Lonergan's second order insight into first order insights. See also Lonergan 1997, chs. 1 and 2.

22 Lonergan 1971, 36–41.

23 On self-correcting process, see Lonergan 1992, 197–8, 311–16, 325–9; Lonergan 1971, 159–60; 208–9.
24 On self-appropriation, see Lonergan 1971, 6–7, 13–16, 83–5; 1974, 213–14; 1992, ch.11, esp. pp. 352–7; 1996, 221–6.
25 *NE* 1113a22–3; also Bk VI, ch. 5.
26 *Posterior Analytics*, Bk II, chs. 1–2.
27 On the unrestricted nature of query directed at being, see Lonergan 1992, 375–5, 659–62.
28 Lonergan 1992, 325.
29 There is no refutation of this in claiming that query can end, say, in despair or utter apathy towards the external world. These are practical and perhaps factual cessations of wonder, query, or concern, but query is in principle still possible. It is only with the attainment of absolute knowledge of all being that query is no longer a possibility. God, for instance, asks no questions.
30 On the pure desire to know, see Lonergan 1992, 372–5. 'Transcendental intending' is a notion that was developed by the later Lonergan in *Method in Theology*. It shares precisely the defining characteristics of the pure desire to know found in his earlier work, *Insight*. Both terms speak of the same a priori orectic orientation towards 'what is to be known,' and for Lonergan this is coextensive with being. See Lonergan 1974, 274.
31 Lonergan 1992, 34, 372. See also '*Insight*: Preface to a Discussion,' in Lonergan 1988, 147: 'It is a desire for ideas, for concepts, for knowledge, but, of itself, it is merely discontented ignorance ... Again, it is not a postulate. Postulates are parts of hypothetical answers, but the desire to know grounds questions. Nor is there any need to postulate questions. They are facts.'
32 Lonergan's understanding of method is as 'a normative pattern of recurrent and related operations yielding cumulative and progressive results. There is a method, then, where there are distinct operations, where each operation is related to the others. Where the set of relations forms a pattern, where the pattern is described as the right way of doing the job, where the operations in accord with the pattern may be repeated indefinitely, and where the fruit of the such repetitions are, not repetitious, but cumulative and progressive' (Lonergan 1971, 4).
33 Lonergan 1992, 404–9
34 This later develops into Lonergan's notion of the transcendental precepts. See Lonergan 1971, 231–2.
35 In this section, I am relying upon much of the summary provided in Doorley 1994, 110–26.
36 See *NE* 1113b24–35, 1114a32–b17.
37 Lonergan 1988, 198.
38 A case in point would be questions and concerns about gravity or radioactivity while living in the Stone Age. These things would never be wondered about nor worried about because they would be beyond anyone's horizon. Nevertheless, gravity and radiation really do affect the reality within which one's horizon is but a heuristic limitation.
39 Lonergan 1993, 88–99.

40 Doorley 1994, 115.

41 Lonergan 1992, ch. 9. Lonergan is indebted to a large degree to the theory of judgment found in Newman 1979; see Lonergan 1996, 237.

42 Lonergan 1992, 59–61, 298–301.

43 A vital essay on this matter is 'The Form of Inference,' in Lonergan 1988, 3–16.

44 Lonergan 1992, 310, 433; 1993, 148.

45 In this case, via what Lonergan calls the 'transcendental precepts,' the exigency that aims at the true and the good – the pure desire to know – commands that whatever we do, we do it circumspectly, rationally, reasonably, and responsibly. These are the general injunctions we use to combat bias. They are checks against the cognitive failures unique to each level of Lonergan's generalized empirical method. See Lonergan 1971, 131–2.

46 There is an important criticism that must lie outside the scope of this project, but which Lonergan spent considerable time answering. For his cognitive method may tell us what we are doing when we are learning and knowing, and it may even be an incorrigible activity of human beings, but the question still remains, why should doing these things get us to the real world, to an objective truth outside of ourselves? Perhaps we are condemned to operate with this method, but why should this method result in attaining to being, to truth, to reality? This is a large question, and here we will have to rely upon the cursory treatment of judgment that I provide as I proceed. For Lonergan's answer to the question, see Lonergan 1992, part 2, chs. 11–13. More discussion on the self-destruction of counter-methods and the self-evident justification of the generalized empirical method is found in Meynell 1998, pt 1.

Chapter 3

1 'Insight is into the concrete world of sense and imagination' and 'the image is necessary for the insight' (Lonergan 1992, 30, 33). Lonergan does not limit *phantasm* to pictorial representations, but includes symbols and descriptions as well. Speaking of mathematical notation, he says, 'The function of symbolism is to supply the relevant image [for insight induction] ... the symbolism constitutes a heuristic technique ... and the effect of apt symbolism is to reduce, if not entirely eliminate, the element of chance [in insight induction]' (42–3). Of course, Lonergan repeats the theme that 'insight is into the data of conscious experience' throughout his work, virtually dedicating his book *Insight* (Lonergan 1992) to this dynamic by citing on his title page this passage from *De Anima*: 'The mind thinks the forms in [*en tois*; dative of means] the *phantasm*' (431b2).

2 See the role of representations in the consciousness of the dramatic subject in Lonergan 1992, 212ff.

3 Lonergan's use of the term 'common sense' is not to be confused with naive realism, with the ideas of the Scottish common sense school, or with the Neo-Thomist doctrine of the grasp of self-evident first principles by common

sense. It is also not in any way related to Aristotle's notion of an internal capacity for unifying the data of the external senses or grasping intentional objects common to more than one sense, such as motion, size, location, and other 'common sensibles.' Lonergan used the word 'common' because this kind of intelligence is found across human history and cultures in all times and places, before and after the higher differentiations of theoretical science and modern empirical science.

4 Lonergan 1992, 200ff.

5 Cf. Wiggins 1978, 146ff.

6 See Lonergan 1971, 40–1. I follow the discussion in Byrne 1997, 72ff.

7 Lonergan 1971, 40–1.

8 For features (i) through (v), see Lonergan 1993, 71ff.; for feature (vi), Lonergan 1992, 198ff.

9 *NE* 1099a7–11.

10 On this provisional restriction of the pure desire to know, see Lonergan 1992, 665.

11 This discussion of patterns of experience is largely derived from Lonergan 1992, ch. 6, though the illustrations are mine.

12 I must clarify an ambiguity that arises when Aristotle and Lonergan speak of 'experience.' For Aristotle, *empeiria*-type experience is an acquired familiarity. On this, Lonergan and Aristotle seem to share a univocal usage. But as was plain the previous chapter, Lonergan also uses 'experience' to mean mental presentations of any kind whatsoever; simply being conscious is to be a subject undergoing some mode of experience. Even with this usage, experience is that which we phenomenally confront in consciousness. All forms of practical experience are also conscious experiences, but not all conscious experience is of the practical.

13 William James (1890, 146–54) posited a general manifold of consciousness in which thought 'is going on' and is in constant flux. By means of attention and inattention we select and deselect parts of that stream, restricting the manifold into a manageable intentional environment. Also, we have an ability to move from *outward* consciousness to *inward* self-consciousness, becoming aware of our inner subjective presence and the various mental operations that we can perform and which are, at least partly, constitutive of conscious experience. Thus, the spontaneous data stream that impinges on us becomes a more truncated flow of consciousness through attention, focus, and the deliberate choices of what stimuli we will allow past the gate, as it were.

14 Lonergan claimed that he did not exhaust the patterns with this list. He allowed for other maximally general ways in which we could construe the data.

15 Lonergan chose the term 'drama' for its primary, non-theatrical meaning: the Greek *drama* is an action, a business, even a duty (from *drao*; to do, be doing, accomplish).

16 See chapter 2, n. 3.

17 Melchin (1987, 143), on the spontaneous emergence of common sense salience selection: '[Our initial] habitual orientations to the objects of expe-

rience are not directly the products of deliberation and choice. Rather, they are by-products or results of one's whole life of common sense decisions and actions. While common sense intelligence has moved on to new matters the subject's orientation to his or her experience has been constituted by previous experiences, insights and decisions.'

18 For instance, during the course of our day, we may deploy philosophic speculation, music appreciation, physical activity, and technical skill. But these modes of intelligence are not arbitrarily activated and incoherently related, for there are intelligent reasons to stop one activity and begin another. There is, then, an overarching mode of intelligence that surreptitiously manages the activation of the others. It provides leadership, as it were; it issues orders and expects actions. This architectonic wisdom that knows what is called for in each actual circumstance is common sense insight.

19 Sherman 1997, 271–2.

20 Dancy 1993, 113.

21 Sherman 1997, 263.

22 The tendency for our conscious intentionality to shift sequentially, and often spontaneously, from one pattern of experience to another, controllable only minimally by self-discipline and concentration, is what Lonergan called the *polymorphic* nature of human consciousness. But patterns of experience can also combine into compounds and dissolve again, so that it is difficult to ascribe dominance to one set of concerns over another. Is the experience of high-speed downhill skiing to be connected to concerns for survival (biological pattern) or play (aesthetic pattern)? Another common example of polymorphism of consciousness is found in our driving home while thinking deeply about some theoretical issue; stop lights and other vehicles are not salient features of our intellectual object; neither is speculative thought a part of driving skill, and yet we effortlessly shift attention between practical and theoretical concerns within the one mind-state of 'driving while thinking.' The notion of the polymorphism of human consciousness refers to this continual combining and shifting of the various patterns of experience and their relative networks of salience. If such polymorphism is a condition of human cognitive operation, then the *phronimos* must perform his excellent function from within that condition.

23 In 'An Interview with Fr. Bernard Lonergan,' Lonergan credits this new emphasis to his reading of Jean Piaget and Susanne Langer and then to the works of Max Scheler and Hildegard von Bingen (Lonergan 1974, 222). Nussbaum cites Pitcher (1965) and Solomon (1976) among the earliest exponents of emotional value cognition. Though an early pioneer of this theory, Lonergan is a virtual unknown because in the 1960s he was working in the much-ignored Catholic university circuit.

24 In the next chapter I will take issue with Nussbaum for losing sight of this distinction.

25 Lonergan 1992, chs. 6–7.

26 Lonergan 1992, 245.

27 See discussion on dramatic bias in Lonergan 1992, 314ff.

28 Lonergan 1992, 215–27.
29 Lonergan 1992, 247.
30 See also Lonergan 1993, 60–2.
31 Lonergan 1992, 251ff.
32 This theme of a universal, yet utterly practical, socio-cultural order is roughed in by Lonergan's discussion of 'cosmopolis' in Lonergan 1992, 263ff. Lonergan's own economic theory is just such an attempt at practical solution; see Lonergan 1998.
33 Lonergan 1992, 251ff. For an excellent discussion of another mode of bias, one that is only touched upon by Lonergan, see Harris 2004, chs. 8–9. Here Harris discusses the pernicious moral and political effects of a kind of *intellectual* bias, what he calls the 'Platonic fallacy' – the reification of the abstract that would think that ideal constructs (i.e., utoptias and other fantasy ideologies) are morally or ontologically superior to concrete world conditions. This bias seems to be intrinsic to intellectuals as a class. Harris places common sense insight and intellectual insight into a counterbalancing dialectic, whereby common sense realism may rightly bring the intellectual back to earth.
34 Sherman 1989, 3.
35 For example, a sound theory should be (i) accurate, (ii) consistent, (iii) broad in scope, (iv) simple, and (v) fruitful. See Kuhn 1977.
36 Kuhn writes, 'Kepler's early election of Copernicanism was due in part to his immersion in the Neoplatonic and Hermetic movements of his day; German Romanticism predisposed those it affected towards both recognition and acceptance of energy conservation; nineteenth-century British social thought had a similar influence on the availability and acceptability of Darwin's concept of struggle for existence' (cited in Kourany 1987, 199).
37 Kuhn 1977.
38 This does not, of course, mean the same *actions* for all people; it is the same *logos*, however, as nicely articulated by Aristotle; see chapter 1, above.
39 For *phronesis* is not interested directly with ethical theory. Good people can hold bad theory and vice versa. Therefore, the plurality of ethical theories is no counter-evidence to there being a unified way of human flourishing. Rather, diversity of theory is by now a much-celebrated part of the overall process of 'coming to know' that defines both Kuhn and Lonergan's work.
40 The full presentation of this line of Lonergan's reasoning is found in Lonergan 1992, ch. 18, 'The Possibility of Ethics.'
41 Sexual orientation theory, for instance, proposes to broaden our understanding of human flourishing by distinguishing the subjective structures of gender identity from biological sex, allowing for a broader range of personal fulfillment than our culture previously could admit. Homosexual flourishing, for instance, would be ruled out if gay orientation is seen as anti–human nature, but orientation theory is changing that. On the other hand, any teleological or functional understanding of biological sex will have to face up to the complementary nature of the opposite sexes and what this indicates about a full account of humanness. Whatever the case may be, the *phronimos*

will be wise at 'playing the cards dealt him' in these matters. One can sense the higher order social good here of a society that tolerates the attempts of persons to make a good life for themselves.

Chapter 4

1 See Nussbaum 2001.
2 For more discussion of what a stricter account would look like, see Leighton 1982; cf. Fortenbaugh 1975.
3 See Nussbaum 1978, and sections in Nussbaum 1986, 1990, and 1994.
4 For a list of differing opinions on this point, see Doorley 1994, 47.
5 This regards Nussbaum 2001, Braman's (1999) critique of Nussbaum notwithstanding.
6 Her own view she calls 'cognitive-evaluative' or simply 'cognitive,' and here she simply means concern with receiving and processing information, not the presence of elaborate calculative, computational, or even reflexive self-aware mechanisms (Nussbaum 2001, 23).
7 Nussbaum 2001, 4.
8 Nussbaum 2001, 27.
9 Nussbaum 2001, 30.
10 Nussbaum 2001, 22.
11 Nussbaum 2001, 23.
12 Nussbaum 2001, 33, 41.
13 Nussbaum 2001, 87, 313–19.
14 Nussbaum 2001, 37.
15 *De Anima,* Bk III, ch. 3.
16 Nussbaum 2001, 38.
17 Nussbaum 2001, 38
18 Nussbaum 2001, 39.
19 Nussbaum 2001, 39ff.
20 Nussbaum 2001, 40.
21 Nussbaum 2001, 43.
22 Some problems, it seems, arise with Nussbaum's view here. For instance, she clearly does claim that her neo-Stoic theory identifies grief with the judgment of personal loss, and hence it is impossible to judge that one has experienced such loss without experiencing grief. But if our emotions were identical with judgments of things deemed to be deeply valuable, then what kind of judgment would we be making when we judge that one of our emotions is, in fact, an *over*-reaction to loss? That judgment would be a more sober assessment of the degree of a thing's personal value to us, but clearly one that need not be another emotion itself. Furthermore, Nussbaum hardly accounts for the judgments whereby I know that I *should* be feeling grief because of deep personal loss, but yet I do not. Here, there is a judgment that losing X is indeed a personal loss, combined with the judgment that a person who loses X should be grieving. But this judgment, while pertaining to real personal value, is not an emotion.

23 Nussbaum 2001, 52.
24 Nussbaum 2001, 47.
25 Nussbaum 2001, 49.
26 Nussbaum 2001, 68.
27 Nussbaum 2001, 72–3.
28 Lonergan 1992, 250ff.
29 Nussbaum 2001, 453.
30 Nussbaum writes, 'We may say, in fact, that the central form of a background emotion is always love or attachment to some thing or person, seen as very important for one's own flourishing – in combination with some general belief to the effect that the well-being of this thing or person is not fully under one's control' (2001, 94).
31 See Nussbaum 1986, 312–17.
32 See *NE*, Bk III, ch. 4ff.; also 1139a21.
33 In *De Anima* 431a7–10, where Aristotle actually makes the distinction between emotional response and judgment, he turns a phrase that McKeon (1941) translates as 'quasi-affirmation' (*hoion kataphasa e apophasa*), which I connect here with prima facie judgment.
34 A fine treatment of Lonergan in this regard is Vertin 1995.
35 Lonergan 1992, 244–69.
36 Lonergan's analysis of dramatic bias led in two directions: as a theory for a new psychoanalytic approach, and as a cognitive impairment theory with which to debate Marxist theories of class struggle. This is discussed in Lonergan 1992 and in Doran 1990. Our concern here is with neither of those directions, but with the influence of dramatic bias upon *phantasm* construal and therefore, on ethical insight induction.
37 Thus for example, in some stone-age cultures, questions regarding the division of labour will simply not arise, or will be ridiculed because 'common sense' dictates that women must nurture and men hunt. The obvious advantages of each sex not only outweigh such questions, but actually mock them as silly and utterly valueless in the game of survival. A future ethics of gender equality will have to wait for the emergence of higher order civilization that removes from the everyday concerns of each group member the exigency of sheer survival. Once the concrete good of physical survival is assured, further questions of quality of life and equity might arise in the context of a more settled and routine social order. But these too will often be raised as practical solution to practical (i.e., social, political, and judicial) problems.
38 Nussbaum 2001, 141–4.
39 Nussbaum 2001, 143.
40 There was a time when the geometric thought of Pythagoras was seen to be as dangerously subversive as is spiritual thought in today's society. 'Eggheads' think little of blue-collar intelligence; artistic thought is seen as a luxury of peace and prosperity, ever vulnerable to budget cuts in favour of more 'practical' needs. The prejudice of one mode of intelligence against another accounts for huge blocks of suppressed insights that may have hampered emergent civilization in quite literally unknowable ways.

41 Nussbaum 2001, 297–456.

42 Nussbaum 2001, 297.

43 As stated before, this is not an exhaustive list of patterns of experience, but if we include Lonergan's category of the phenomenological pattern (interiority) and the religious pattern, we probably have most of them.

44 I think this is what Lawrence Blum captures when he claims that impartialist views (Kantians and consequentialists) and particularist views (virtue ethics) of the human good are not reducible to each other or to some more fundamental ethical theory of viewpoint, for 'there is no unitary *moral point of view* that can be defined in terms of a single moral notion or procedure.' He echoes Aristotle's view that there are properly basic human goods, and they are not commensurable: partialist loyalty to one's family is basic, as is impartiality in judicial procedure. See Hooker and Little 2000, 206.

45 The orientation of the questions of the intellectual pattern of experience is ultimately ontological, towards being itself. If permitted to operate without bias, intellect is capable of asking every question about every thing. Thus, its horizon is being itself, an unrestricted notion. Still, ethics is more than knowing, and unrestricted questions regarding being are not yet unrestricted desires for the good, and so we are looking for some further openness that regards human objects of desire, choice, and action.

46 Lonergan 1971, 131, 235–6.

47 Lonergan 1971, 31–2. A good discussion of care and its impact upon *phantasm* and the questions of value we would ask is in Melchin 1993, 215–28.

48 Lonergan 1993, 88–91.

49 Lonergan 1993, 91.

50 This sheds light upon how bias impacts the horizon limits of various patterns of experience. For bias will be seen as a truncation of love, compassion, and concern – love here defined as unlimited goodwill and concern towards others, or the valuing of others with that same intensity that one values oneself. Bias is always a preservation of self-interest precisely at the expense of the best interest of another (person or group). On proper self-love according to Aristotle, see *NE*, Bk IX, chs. 4 and 8.

51 Lonergan's notion of humans as real values in themselves seems to be essentially the Kantian notion of humans as ends in themselves. See discussion in Lonergan 1971, 31, 50–1.

52 Lonergan 1971, 105–6.

53 'But a rounded moral judgment is ever the work of a fully developed self-transcending subject or, as Aristotle would put it, of a virtuous man' (Lonergan's note to *NE* 1105b5–8, 1106b36ff., Lonergan 1971, 41).

54 Nussbaum 2001, 453–4.

55 Nussbaum 2001, 474ff.

56 Nussbaum 2001, 479ff. The last of these principles – compassion – is also defined by the cognitive content that must be rightly balanced in its judgments: seriousness of circumstance, appropriate judgments of blame and responsibility, and appropriate extent and limitation of its concern. See pp. 414ff.

57 Nussbaum 2001, 480–1.
58 Nussbaum 2001, 480–1.
59 Nussbaum 2004, 479.
60 'Aristotle in a general way accepts an account of emotion that is not unlike my own. He does, however, hold that love – or at least *philia* – is not merely an emotion. Although it involves emotion, it also has requirements that go beyond the emotional ... in a reciprocal relationship of Aristotle's sort, the emotions involved a conception of the object as a person who wants and actively seeks my good, and for whom I both want and actively seek the good' (Nussbaum 2001, 474; see also p. 498. On Aristotle and compassion, see pp. 306, 393).
61 Lonergan 1971, 289.
62 Lonergan 1993, 91. On the other hand, that bias blocks charity; see Lonergan 1971, 284.
63 See 'Emotions and Infancy,' Nussbaum 2001, ch. 4.
64 Lonergan 1993, 91.
65 The description of this phenomenological fact is not usually found in philosophical texts, and that is why Nussbaum herself has turned to literature and narrative to capture it.
66 Cf. *NE*, Bk IX, ch. 12.
67 Clearly, there are countless other dangers to the good and the right posed by the actions done in the name of love. This subject is covered throughout Nussbaum 2001 and is an endless subject in literature and poetry. Like any other passion, if not trained towards the mean between extremes, as Aristotle taught, an emotion such as love may become an impediment to the human good. But this is not what is in dispute. The objection I am dealing with claims that family love will necessarily be *un*objective; that is, it will unduly distort salience in favour of one's loved ones, and this is of the very essence of familial love and loyalty. Thus, family love may be a bias that we want to keep.
68 Nussbaum argues that background love is an emotion nevertheless, for though we do not feel it, the emotion explains our actions and reactions in various contexts. Her example, used above, is fear of writing exams. Another example might be the overall levity that is not explicitly felt at the staff party, but which shapes the things we allow ourselves to say and do that otherwise might be unacceptable.

Concluding Summary

1 Especially her *De Anima* studies (Nussbaum and Rorty 1992). See also Nussbaum 1978 and 1986.
2 The clearest modern restatement of the Aristotelian position on this vital point is found in Adler 1991.

References

Ackrill, J.L. 1973. *Aristotle's Ethics*. London: Faber and Faber.

– 1981. *Aristotle the Philosopher*. Oxford: Oxford University Press.

Adler, M.J. 1991. *Desires, Right and Wrong*. New York: MacMillan.

Allan, D.J. 1955. 'The Practical Syllogism.' In *Autour d'Aristote*, ed. S. Mansion, 325–40. Louvain: Publications universitaires de Louvain.

Annas, J. 1993. *The Morality of Happiness*. Oxford: Oxford University Press.

Braman, B. 1999. 'Mutilating Desire? Lonergan and Nussbaum: A Dialectical Encounter.' *Method: A Journal of Lonergan Studies* 17:1–26.

Brentano, F. 1969. *The Origin of Our Knowledge of Right and Wrong*. New York: Humanities Press.

Burnyeat, M.F. 1980. 'Aristotle on Learning to be Good.' In Rorty 1980, 69–92.

Byrne, P. 1997. '*Phronesis* and Common Sense Judgment: Aristotle and Lonergan on Moral Wisdom.' *Proceedings of the American Catholic Philosophical Quarterly* 71:3–78.

Cassidy, J.P. 1996. 'Extending Bernard Lonergan's Ethics.' PhD diss., University of Ottawa.

Cooper, J. 1975. *Reason and the Human Good*. Cambridge, MA: Harvard University Press.

Dahl, N.O. 1984. *Practical Reason, Aristotle, and Weakness of the Will*. Minneapolis: University of Minnesota Press.

Dancy, J. 1991. 'Intuitionism.' In Singer 1991, 411–20.

– 1993. *Moral Reasons*. Oxford: Blackwell.

DesAutels, P. 1996. 'Gestalt Shifts in Moral Perception.' In *Minds and Morals: Essays on Ethics and Cognitive Science*, ed. L. May, M. Friedman, and A. Clark, 129–43. Cambridge, MA: MIT Press.

DeMoss, D.J. 1990. 'Acquiring Ethical Ends.' *Ancient Philosophy* 10:63–79.

Doorley, M. 1994. 'The Role of Feelings in the Ethical Intentionality Analysis of Bernard Lonergan.' PhD diss., Boston College.

Doran, R.M. 1990. *Theology and the Dialectics of History.* Toronto: University of Toronto Press.

Dreyfus, H., and S. Dreyfus. 1990. 'What is Morality? A Phenomenological Account of the Development of Ethical Expertise.' In *Universalism vs. Communitarianism: Contemporary Debate in Ethics,* ed. D. Rasmussen, 237–64. Cambridge, MA: MIT Press.

Dunne, J. 1993. *Back to the Rough Ground: Toward a Post-Critical Philosophy.* Notre Dame, IN: University of Notre Dame Press.

Engberg-Pedersen, T. 1983. *Aristotle's Theory of Moral Insight.* Oxford: Clarendon.

Frede, D. 1992. 'The Cognitive Role of *Phantasia* in Aristotle.' In Nussbaum and Rorty 1992, 279–95.

Fortenbaugh, W.W. 1975. *Aristotle on Emotions.* London: Duckworth.

Gauthier, R.A., and J.Y. Jolif, trans. and ed. 1970. *L'éthique à Nicomaque.* 2nd ed. Louvain: Publications universitaires de Louvain.

Gick, M.L., and S.J. McGarry. 1992. 'Learning from Mistakes: Inducing Analogous Solution Failures to a Source Problem Produces Later Successes in Analogical Transfer.' *Journal of Experimental Psychology: Learning, Memory and Cognition* 18:623–39.

Gomez-Lobo, A. 1995. 'Aristotle's Right Reason.' In *Aristotle, Virtue and the Mean,* ed. R. Bosley, R. Shirier, and J. Sisson. *Apeiron* 25:15–34.

Greenwood, L.H.G., trans. 1909. *Nicomachean Ethics. Book Six, with Essay, Notes, and Translation.* Repr. New York: Arno Press, 1973.

Grote, G. 1890. *Aristotle.* Repr. New York: Arno Press, 1973.

Gruber, H.E. 1995. 'Insight and Affect in the History of Science.' In *The Nature of Insight,* ed. R.J. Sternberg and J.E. Davidson, 397–432. Cambridge, MA: MIT Press.

Hankinson R.J. 1990. 'Perception and Evaluation: Aristotle on the Moral Imagination.' *Dialogue* 29:41–63.

Harris, L. 2004. *Civilization and Its Enemies.* New York: Free Press.

Hett, W.S., trans. 1936. *On the Soul.* Loeb Classical Library. Repr. Cambridge, MA: Harvard University Press, 1995.

Hooker, B., and M. Little. 2000. *Moral Particularism.* Oxford: Clarendon.

Irwin, T.H. 1981. 'Aristotle's Method of Ethics.' In *Studies in Aristotle,* ed. D.J. O'Meara, 193–223. Washington, DC: Catholic University of America Press.

– trans. 1985. *Aristotle's 'Nicomachean Ethics.'* Indianapolis, IN: Hackett.

– 2000. 'Ethics as an Inexact Science: Aristotle's Ambitions for Moral Theory.' In *Moral Particularism,* ed. B. Hooker and M. Little, 100–29. Oxford: Clarendon.

Jaeger, W. 1939. *Paideia: The Ideals of Greek Culture.* Trans. Gilbert Highet. 3 vols. Oxford: Oxford University Press.

James, W. 1890. *The Principles of Psychology.* Repr. Chicago: University of Chicago Press, 1984.

Kaplan, C.A., and H.A. Simon. 1990. 'In Search of Insight.' *Cognitive Psychology* 22:374–419.

Keller, H. 1904. *The Story of My Life.* Repr. New York: Dell, 1961.

Kourany, J. 1987. *Scientific Knowledge: Basic Issues in the Philosophy of Science.* Belmont, CA: Wadsworth.

Kuhn, T.S. 1977. *The Essential Tension: Selected Studies in Scientific Tradition and Change.* Chicago: University of Chicago Press.

Leighton, S.R. 1982. 'Aristotle and the Emotions.' *Phronesis* 27:144–74.

Lonergan, B.J.F. 1968. *The Subject.* Milwaukee, WI: Marquette University Press.

– 1971. *Method in Theology.* New York: Herder and Herder. Repr. Toronto: University of Toronto Press, 1990.

– 1974. *A Second Collection.* Ed. W. Ryan and B. Tyrrell. Philadelphia: Westminster.

– 1988. *Collection: Papers by Bernard Lonergan.* 2nd ed. Vol. 4 of *Collected Works of Bernard Lonergan,* ed. F.E. Crowe and R.M. Doran. Toronto: University of Toronto Press.

– 1990. *Understanding and Being.* 2nd ed., ed. E.A. Morelli and M.D. Morelli. Vol. 5 of *Collected Works of Bernard Lonergan,* ed. F.E. Crowe and R.M. Doran. Toronto: University of Toronto Press.

– 1992. *Insight: A Study of Human Understanding.* 5th ed. Vol. 3 of *Collected Works of Bernard Lonergan,* ed. F.E. Crowe and R.M. Doran. Toronto: University of Toronto Press.

– 1993. *Topics in Education.* Vol. 10 of *Collected Works of Bernard Lonergan,* ed. F.E. Crowe and R.M. Doran. Toronto: University of Toronto Press.

– 1996. *Philosophical and Theological Papers 1958–1964.* Vol. 6 of *Collected Works of Bernard Lonergan,* ed. F.E. Crowe and R.M. Doran. Toronto: University of Toronto Press.

– 1997. *Verbum.* Vol. 2 of *Collected Works of Bernard Lonergan,* ed. F.E. Crowe and R.M. Doran. Toronto: University of Toronto Press.

– 1998. *For a New Political Economy.* Ed. P. McShane. Vol. 21 of *Collected Works of Bernard Lonergan,* ed. F.E. Crowe and R.M. Doran. Toronto: University of Toronto Press.

Louden, R. 1986. 'Aristotle's Practical Particularism.' *Ancient Philosophy* 6:123–38.

Mackie, J.L. 1977. *Ethics: Inventing Right and Wrong.* New York: Penguin.

McDowell, J. 1979. 'Virtue and Reason.' *Monist* 62:331–50.

– 1996. 'Deliberation and Moral Development in Aristotle's Ethics.' In *Aristotle, Kant, and the Stoics,* ed. S. Engstrom and J. Whiting, 19–34. Cambridge: Cambridge University Press.

McKeon, R. ed. 1941. *The Basic Works of Aristotle.* New York: Random House.

Melchin, K.R. 1987. *History, Ethics, and Emergent Probability.* Lanham, MD: University Press of America.

– 1993. 'Moral Decision-Making and the Role of the Moral Question.' *Method: A Journal of Lonergan Studies* 11:215–28.

Meynell, H.A. 1998. *Redirecting Philosophy.* Toronto: University of Toronto Press.

Monan, J.D. 1968. *Moral Knowledge and Its Methodology in Aristotle.* Oxford: Clarendon.

Moore, G.E. 1903. *Principia Ethica.* London: Cambridge University Press.

Morelli, M.D., and E.A Morelli. 1997. *The Lonergan Reader.* Toronto: University of Toronto Press.

Nagel, T. 1972. 'Aristotle on *Eudaimonia.*' *Phronesis* 17:252–9.

Newman, J.H. 1979. *An Essay in Aid of a Grammar of Assent.* Notre Dame, IN: University of Notre Dame Press.

Nussbaum, M.C. 1978. *Aristotle's 'De motu animalium.'* Princeton: Princeton University Press.

– 1986. *The Fragility of Goodness.* Cambridge: Cambridge University Press.

– 1990. *Love's Knowledge: Essays on Philosophy and Literature.* New York: Oxford University Press.

– 1994. *The Therapy of Desire: Theory and Practice in Hellenistic Ethics.* Princeton: Princeton University Press.

– 1995. 'Aristotle on Human Nature and the Foundation of Ethics.' In *World, Man, and Ethics: Essays on the Ethical Philosophy of Bernard Williams,* ed. J.E.J. Altham and R. Harrison, 86–131. Cambridge: Cambridge University Press.

– 2001. *Upheavals of Thought: The Intelligence of Emotions.* Cambridge: Cambridge University Press.

Nussbaum, M.C., and A.O. Rorty, eds. 1992. *Essays on Aristotle's 'De anima.'* Oxford: Clarendon.

Peterson, S. 1992. 'Apparent Circularity in Aristotle's Account of Right Action in the *Nicomachean Ethics.*' *Apeiron* 25:83–107.

Philippe, M.D. 1971. '*Phantasia* in the Philosophy of Aristotle.' *Thomist* 35:1–42.

Pitcher, G. 1965. 'Emotion.' *Mind* 74:326–46.

Poincaré, H. 1952. *Science and Hypothesis.* New York: Dover.

Polanyi, M. 1958. *Personal Knowledge.* Chicago: University of Chicago Press.

Rackham, H., trans. 1926. *Nicomachean Ethics.* Loeb Classical Library. Repr. Cambridge, MA: Harvard University Press, 1982.

Rawls, J. 1971. *A Theory of Justice.* Cambridge, MA: Harvard University Press.

Richardson, H.S. 1992. 'Desire and the Good in *De anima.*' In Nussbaum and Rorty 1992, 381–99.

Rorty, A.O., ed. 1980. *Essays on Aristotle's Ethics.* London: Duckworth.

– ed. 1996. *Essays on Aristotle's Rhetoric.* Berkeley and Los Angeles: University of California Press.

Ross, W.D. 1930. *The Right and the Good.* Oxford: Clarendon.

Schooler, J.W, S. Ohlsson, K. Brooks. 1993. 'Thoughts beyond Words: When Language Overshadows Insight.' *Journal of Experimental Psychology: General* 122:166–83.

Schuchman, P. 1980. *Aristotle and the Problem of Moral Discernment.* Frankfurt: Peter D. Lang.

Sherman, N. 1989. *The Fabric of Character: Aristotle's Theory of Virtue.* Oxford: Clarendon.

– 1997. *Making a Necessity of Virtue: Aristotle and Kant on Virtue.* Cambridge: Cambridge University Press.

Sidgwick, H. 1907. *The Methods of Ethics.* London: MacMillan and Company. Repr. New York: Dover, 1966.

Simonton, D.K. 1984. 'Artistic Creativity and Interpersonal Relationships across and within Generations.' *Journal of Personality and Social Psychology* 46:1273–86.

Singer, P. ed. 1991. *A Companion to Ethics.* Oxford: Blackwell.

Smyth, H.W. 1956. *Greek Grammar.* Cambridge, MA: Harvard University Press.

Solomon, R.C. 1976. *The Passions: Emotions and the Meaning of Life.* 2nd ed. Indianapolis, IN: Hackett.

Sorabji, R. 1980. 'Aristotle and the Role of Intellect in Virtue.' In Rorty 1980, 201–21.

Sternberg, R.J., and J.E. Davidson, eds. 1995. *The Nature of Insight.* Cambridge, MA: MIT Press.

Striker, G. 1996. 'Emotions in Context: Aristotle's Treatment of the Passion in the *Rhetoric* and His Moral Psychology.' In Rorty 1996, 207–19.

Tye, Michael. 1991. *The Imagery Debate,* Cambridge, MA: MIT Press.

Urmson, J.O. 1988. *Aristotle's Ethics.* Oxford: Basil Blackwell.

Vertin, M. 1995. 'Judgment of Value for the Later Lonergan.' *Method: A Journal of Lonergan Studies* 13:221–48.

Vitruvius. 1914. *The Ten Books of Architecture.* Trans. M.H. Morgan. Cambridge, MA: Harvard University Press.

Wallace, D.B. 1991. 'The Genesis and Microgenesis of Sudden Insight in the Creation of Literature.' *Creativity Research Journal* 4:41–50.

Walsh, M.M. 1999. 'The Role of Universal Knowledge in Aristotelian Moral Virtue.' *Ancient Philosophy* 19:73–88.

Wedin, M.V. 1988. *Mind and Imagination in Aristotle.* New Haven: Yale University Press.

Weisberg, R. 1992. *Creativity: Beyond the Myth of Genius.* New York: W.H. Freeman.

Wiggins, D. 1978. 'Deliberation and Practical Reason.' In *Practical Reasoning,* ed. J. Raz, 144–52. Oxford: Oxford University Press.

Woods, M, trans. 1982. *Aristotle's Eudemian Ethics, Books I, II, and VIII.* Oxford: Clarendon.

Zsambock, C.E., and G. Klein, eds. 1997. *Naturalistic Decision Making.* Mahwah, NJ: Lawrence Erlbaum.

Index